Life Beyond Suicide

For all who have lost loved ones to suicide
or who have thought of ending their own lives;
with love and light

Life Beyond Suicide

Reflections on Loss and Love

Edited by

Samuel Wells, Ann Feloy
and David Mosse

CANTERBURY
PRESS

© Samuel Wells, Ann Feloy and David Mosse 2025

Published in 2025 by Canterbury Press

Editorial office
3rd Floor, Invicta House,
110 Golden Lane,
London EC1Y 0TG, UK
www.scmpress.co.uk

Canterbury Press is an imprint of Hymns Ancient & Modern Ltd
(a registered charity)

Hymns Ancient & Modern®

Hymns Ancient & Modern® is a registered trademark of
Hymns Ancient & Modern Ltd
13A Hellesdon Park Road, Norwich,
Norfolk NR6 5DR, UK

All rights reserved. No part of this publication may be reproduced,
stored in a retrieval system, or transmitted,
in any form or by any means, electronic, mechanical,
photocopying or otherwise, without the prior permission of
the publisher, Canterbury Press.

The editors and contributors have asserted the right under the Copyright, Designs
and Patents Act 1988 to be identified as the Author of this Work

Scripture quotations are from New Revised Standard Version Bible: Anglicized
Edition, copyright © 1989, 1995 National Council of the Churches of Christ in
the United States of America. Used by permission. All rights reserved worldwide.

British Library Cataloguing in Publication data

A catalogue record for this book is available
from the British Library

ISBN: 978-1-78622-651-8

EU GPSR Authorised Representative
LOGOS EUROPE, 9 rue Nicolas Poussin, 17000, LA ROCHELLE, France
E-mail: Contact@logoseurope.eu

No part of this book may be used or reproduced in any manner for the
purpose of training artificial intelligence technologies or systems.

Typeset by Regent Typesetting

Contents

Preface   vii

Part One

1. Gathering to Find Hope   3
   David Mosse

2. Life Beyond Suicide   9
   Ann Feloy

Part Two

3. Losing a Child   19
   Contributors

4. Losing a Loved One   40
   Contributors

5. Losing the Will to Live   59
   Contributors

6. Walking Alongside   73
   Contributors

7. Finding Solidarity on the Journey After Suicide   79
   David Mosse

8. Steps Toward Faith   91
   Samuel Wells

Part Three

9 Faith in the Face of Suicide   111
   Samuel Wells

10 Ideas for Preparing Your Own 'Time Together' Service   125
   Ann Feloy

11 Personal and Public Prayer   135
   Samuel Wells

Appendix: Reflective Practices   141

Preface

It's long been a motto of mine that if you can't make it happy, make it beautiful. That's perhaps never truer than when it comes to living beyond suicide. Some find that suicide takes away words: there's nothing to say. For many, grief is profoundly isolating: there's nowhere to find comfort. Loss can be deeply shattering: it can feel like there's no meaning, truth or wisdom to bring to it. But that's not everyone's experience. The depth of sorrow can deepen friendships and disclose profound truths. Some find they move towards acceptance and discover consolation and hope, deep as the grief may be. Everyone has their own story to tell. Life beyond suicide also refers to the complex emotions – sometimes conflicted, other times tentative – of those who are themselves thinking or have contemplated or indeed have survived a suicide attempt. The pain of those bereaved through suicide may put them at greater risk of having thoughts of suicide themselves.

Which is why it's an initiative of great courage to seek to find words, to bring people together, and tentatively to offer beauty in the midst of such unique suffering. That is what David Mosse did in 2015 when he conceived the notion of an annual service for those affected by suicide, and what his team of advisers and organizers did by bringing the service about at St Martin-in-the-Fields for the first time. Among those original collaborators were Clare Milford Haven, Hamish Elvidge and Amy Meadows. The service, which has taken place each year since, seeks to give space, silence and gentle respect to enable participants and attendees to find companionship, truth and hope. Both the service and the reception that follows are a unique moment when one doesn't need to resort to small talk but can simply share from heart and soul about things everyone there knows.

This book is an attempt to record in words the spirit of that service and to offer to a wider circle many of the thoughts that have been shared there. These testimonies form the middle part of the book. The first part offers the rationale behind this initiative – now a movement, with replica services elsewhere – offered by David, the founder, and Ann Feloy, who now runs the service. David has spoken at most of the services, and I have spoken at all of them, so there is a chapter each in the second part for our respective addresses. The book concludes with theological reflections and resources for those who might find it helpful to consider the more explicitly Christian aspects of the event, which are generally kept low-key on the day. There is also an appendix with a selection of reflective practices.

Thanks are due to those who have assisted in organizing the service, all who have spoken and sung, those from the team at St Martin's who have supported the occasion, all who have offered support and resources on the day, and St Martin's Voices, directed by Andrew Earis, who have sung each year. Sincere thanks to Jane Ware who assisted in liaising with contributors and preparing the manuscript. And special thanks to all who have found in themselves the courage to tell their story.

We would be glad to hear from readers who may be considering holding a 'Time Together' service so we can join forces to create a truly incredible event, sharing our love and light simultaneously. Please contact Ann at ann@ollysfuture.org.uk to talk about the next steps and how to make it beautiful on the day. If you would like to work collaboratively, for example holding your service at the same time as the London service, or in the same week, the charity Olly's Future can supply you with the artwork for the logos for the 'Time Together' service. You can read more about past services and hear audio recordings of them at https://ollysfuture.org.uk/st-martin-in-the-fields-service. We are deeply grateful to all who volunteer their time to help Olly's Future with the running of the event and to all the wonderful charities that support us every year by having a stand afterwards at the reception. It is a privilege to hold this event. We are seeking to do something to help ease the pain and suffering of others.

Our hope is that in reading these words, those affected by suicide may find beauty in the face of grief, isolation, horror and sorrow.

Samuel Wells
February 2025

Part One

I

Gathering to Find Hope

DAVID MOSSE

Every year since March 2015 there has been a service of reflection at St Martin-in-the-Fields in Trafalgar Square in the heart of London for people affected by suicide. People have been invited to 'a time together with music, words and space for reflection for those living with loss and grief, and journeying towards hope and healing'. While held in a famously beautiful church and involving sacred music that reaches into our hearts, these are not billed as or understood by most participants as explicitly religious events; they welcome people of all and no faith, and bring poems, songs and testimonies from different traditions responding to the pain of suicide.

Outside, in Trafalgar Square, the traffic and Saturday crowds buzz around, and many who come to the services are themselves busy with the tireless work of grieving, or activism in suicide prevention. But inside, the church offers a space apart and time for contemplation and being with others for a moment of shared reflection. We lend our thoughts and our feelings to music carried in the voices of the choir, allowing a kind of harmonization of the many individual sorrows, regrets and hopes.

The initiative came from members of a group of suicide prevention charities (The Alliance of Suicide Prevention Charities, TASC), many started by families who felt compelled to do something in the wake of the loss of a dearly loved person to suicide, and working to raise awareness to better reach those in suicidal crisis and support those bereaved by suicide. Of course, for many, working to make our communities, organizations and society safer from suicide is also a way of grieving, of not being alone, and bearing witness to the fact of suicide and the need to act to prevent avoidable deaths. In the context of such shared action, the 6,000 such deaths recorded each year, and the consequent individual grief and private trauma, fuels calls for political and policy action. But as I approached my own landmark of five years from the death of my son, Jake, I felt that we should come together with others, not only to *do* but also to *be*; to face together the enormity of suicide, and what it means for us individually and collectively. This meant bringing together those who experience the loss and pain of bereavement and those who know such pain from having been suicidal or attempting to end their life. The 'Time to Talk' (now 'Time Together') service was born from that impulse to find a still point; a place to listen and be with the anguish of suicide.

I don't think any of us can make sense of suicide, because at its centre is something unknowable. This is what lies behind the tormenting question, 'Why?', asked by so many bereaved. Those who share their experience say, as I have, that to begin with, there's no meaning, no narrative, not even language – just an animal howl. The event and its discovery are too enormous and terrible to take in or give shape to. But finding a way to think about, or find a story for, the death of my child by his own hand is a requirement of living with that awful fact, of rebuilding the story of my life, and recovering my place in the world. And so it is for many others too.

But the stories we tell tend to place ourselves – what we did or said, or did not do or say – at the centre so as to produce terrible guilt; or maybe it is floating guilt that builds these stories for us. But in time, we may allow other narratives to emerge as we struggle to preserve the memory of those dear to us and our relationship of love, and to preserve ourselves from the impulse and anxiety of self-blame.

By being with others, we find witnesses to our tragedy and listen to those whose similar struggles we recognize. We may come to see a pattern and realize that ours is not a singularity but a *kind* of experience. My individual, subjective and fragmented experience – perhaps of trauma that had no words – acquires language and social recognition. And through compassion for others whose experience I share, I learn to be kinder to myself, and blame myself less.

In the 'Time Together' services and the fellowship that surrounds them, people make connections born of the kinship of grief, experience mutual recognition, lend and borrow from each other's sense-making, and re-cast individual tragedies as collective ones. Loss is borne and hope made through connections. It counters the profound detachment and disconnection that suicide and loss involves, and the social stigma that may surround suicide.

When we say that suicide is unspeakable, this is also because it is surrounded by fear, judgement, even criminality, preserved in the language of having 'committed' suicide. If stigma means anything here, it is that the anxiety that suicide provokes – the pre-emptive explanations or the judgements it attracts – affects social interactions, as people draw invisible lines between their ordinary selves and lives, and the suicide. Some of this is in the mind of the bereaved (a self-stigmatizing projection), but society has placed it there. It may take years, decades, perhaps a lifetime, before a parent can say to someone in an ordinary walk of life, without anxiety, 'My son killed himself'; or my mother, my sister, my husband, my friend; as if this were a tragic accident or fatal illness. Time Together services may help protect from the kind of moral injury that can be inflicted on those bereaved and those who have made attempts on their own lives. As such, the services are socially and politically significant as well as individually meaningful. This task is also carried by the suicide prevention and bereavement support organizations who join in the reception after the service.

Gathered in this book are the testimonies of those who bring themselves and their experiences, not trying to explain or offer answers, but bringing compassion, self-compassion and human connection. These brave words show loss in many forms and painted in many colours – loss of self and of loved ones. Loss is profound, visceral, existential. How could it not be when the loss is experienced as the loss of a part of oneself? This grief is experienced in mind and body, and we see how lonely it can be. The wounds it bestows are precious and integral, like the love they show. And precious too are the words of these testimonies.

Suicide is almost always experienced as a shock, even where foreseen within a long struggle with a tormented life, through which the love of a parent or spouse has endured beyond hopelessness. Behind many stories of death by suicide is another one, less commonly told, of how family members and friends were able to keep their loved ones alive for so long, despite the odds, the many attempts, the long illness and exhausting commitment to living.

The testimonies show us the terrible legacy of suicide. Suicide is a death unlike any other because it is a death with a different relationship to the living. This is coded in cultural and historical practice. We may not pile heavy stones atop the grave to stop the spirit rising, but those grieving such a death still recognize, in other terms, that 'such a terrible act would come back and infect the living.'[1] The psychiatrist Rachel Gibbons writes of suicide as an 'acting out' that substitutes actions for

---

1 D. Campbell and R. Hale, 2017, *Working in the Dark: Understanding the Pre-Suicide State of Mind*, London: Routledge, p. 8.

extreme, painful feelings, and that with this behaviour 'painful aspects of the deceased's internal world are projected into those left behind. In this way others are implicated in this enactment', burdened with responsibility beyond reality.[2]

There can be a compulsion to find a way to be close to those lost, to know what took them away, what might have saved them. Those grieving may find themselves entering the darkness, loss and guilt of the loved ones they are trying to understand – one of several ways in which suicide is contagious. It is easy to lose one's way. This is why testimony from those who have been suicidal and close to death but survived is so valuable and strangely comforting. Indeed, maybe there is a particular connection and intimacy between those who open up their experience of being suicidal and those who are vulnerable in their grief. Compassion and companionship of this kind is held in the Time Together services.

We are privileged that those who have come close to death share their experience. We hear the suicidal state described, not just as intense emotional pain beyond capacity to cope, but as disconnection, even from those we love: absence, death inside, loss of self-reality, numbness or being in a bubble. Inescapable. What is particularly hard to hear is the shame brought with suicidal thoughts, the self-blame, self-loathing or anger at failure, or being broken beyond repair. Such despair is experienced as outside the reach of love from others; and from one speaker we hear that their suicidal mind believed they had become such a burden to the family that suicide would be an act of love.

Like the immediate grief of loss, the suicidal state has no words. It is unfathomable, even to those who come to speak about their attempts to die that, miraculously, they survived. It makes no sense. Equally mysterious is the moment, maybe an epiphany, when life is grasped again, when re-connection allows someone to learn to reinhabit life.[3] The will to live and the will to die may not be poles apart, but mutually uncomprehending (or unknown) parts of one person. Many who grieve a lost dear one know they heard and saw the part that intended to live, while an unknown part was planning their death. Or, maybe holding to life in the face of the indescribable dread of depression becomes impossible.

---

2 Rachel Gibbons, 2024, 'Understanding the Psychodynamics of the Pathway to Suicide', *International Review of Psychiatry*, DOI: 10.1080/09540261.2024.2351937.

3 Neil Armstrong, 2024, *Collaborative Ethnographic Working in Mental Health: Knowledge, Power and Hope in an Age of Bureaucratic Accountability*, London: Routledge, p. 92.

One of our most inspiring contributors, Gill Hayes, survived a near-lethal suicide attempt, and went on to campaign and give the power of hope to those suffering serious depression. Tragically, Gill took her own life two years after she spoke at the service. Gill's family wanted her inspiring talk to be included in this book, and not gloss over the tragic death of a brave and loving woman, wife and mother, whose passion for life was real and the love of her family deep. It is a heartrending truth that the struggle to stay alive for some who show the greatest imaginable courage can be overwhelmed by the intolerable torment of severe depression returning.

This collection of voices heard at St Martin's also includes clinicians and volunteers whose work is to listen and respond, to 'walk alongside' those in suicidal crisis. It requires a special skill, kindness and compassion to stay with the uncertainty that surrounds a person who is suicidal; to be present as a human companion, to listen without judgement or fear. As one of the chaplains at Beachy Head told my colleague Rachel Gibbons, 'To help a truly suicidal person you have to approach them with an open heart ... If you are worried about the risk their action poses to you, they are more likely to jump.' To be open-hearted is to trust, despite not knowing what will happen, to hold hope for another by finding connection as a fellow human, to be vulnerable and allow oneself to be seen as well as to listen. Trust may be necessary for someone to regain control and rebuild a life from having been on the edge. This is the opposite of the fear-driven efforts to assert control over a person seen as at risk of suicidal behaviour, or the detachment of professional clinical distance and risk management. And clinicians have to carry that 'not knowing' in the event of a death by suicide, holding on to integrity and honesty in the painful mix of responsibility and sadness that ensues.

Many of us profoundly affected by suicide are drawn to what we fear most; to understand, to intervene, to prevent this terrible outcome. I cannot relinquish suicide; I still grieve for the manner of my son's death. Indeed, with all its unanswered questions, suicide is also a commission to me, and as witnessed in these testimonies, to many others who continue to care for those they lost, feeling an unbidden responsibility to act for those who face the peril of suicide. For some, the faithfulness to the tragic event[4] that suicide engenders brings unresolved grief, a world

---

4 T. Kuan, 2017, 'The Problem of Moral Luck, Anthropologically Speaking', *Anthropological Theory* 17 (1), pp. 30–59, p. 54.

forever terrifyingly full of impending disaster; at worst it brings further suicide.

But for others, knowing the worst that can happen changes the scale of what is important, turning what threatens to deplete the self into a project of self-making, into new energy and drive for life by means of engagement in the world of suicide prevention. Perhaps action here is more than a means to an end; it is a way to give meaning to a loss that threatens to be unbearable. Perhaps at a deep level we are – I am – involved in experiments with time, and with hope, a 'temporality of second chances',[5] for we know personally that the terrible outcome against which all action is oriented has already happened; all beginnings start with the ending of an unalterable plotline.[6]

At least, I might say that the inalterability of personal tragedy draws me to a world that promises to be alterable through suicide prevention. Some of us enter into the very health or other systems that failed (us) in order to bring alertness and change from the perspective of how wrong things can go. We retrace and overwrite the pathways to tragedy with hope, exemplified in the many suicide prevention innovations we learn about in these pages, driven by families out of their own tragedies. These are living memorials.

But working in suicide prevention is unavoidably paradoxical. When we sit with 'experts' planning interventions to save lives, to manage risk, we also know from personal tragedy that risk was not managed, signs did not warn; that we are not in control of the things that matter most. We bring to the table our full awareness of existential vulnerability, the knowledge that life is unstable, chaotic and cruel, which perhaps is itself, as Arthur Kleinman puts it, 'a kind of quiet liberation, preparing for new ways of being ourselves, living in the world and making a difference in the lives of others.'[7] And sometimes we – those affected by suicide – just need to come together silently to bear witness to the fact of suicide and all that it means. And this is the continuing value of 'Time Together'.

---

[5] Veena Das, 2007, *Life and Words: Violence and the Descent into the Ordinary*, Berkeley, CA: University of California Press, p. 101.

[6] Cherly Mattingly, 2013, 'Moral Selves and Moral Scenes: Narrative Experiments in Everyday Life', *Ethnos* 78 (3), pp. 301–27, p. 318.

[7] Arthur Kleinman, 2006, *What Really Matters: Living a Moral Life Amidst Uncertainty and Danger*, Oxford and New York: Oxford University Press, p. 10.

2

Life Beyond Suicide

ANN FELOY

In 2022 I was privileged to be invited to give a testimony at Time Together at St-Martin-in-the-Fields about losing my son Oliver – Olly to all his friends. Little did I suspect that the following year, the charity we formed in memory of my son, Olly's Future, would take over the running of the event, continuing the beautiful service that David Mosse and other bereaved parents established in 2015.

It is humbling to acknowledge that since it began, thousands of people have gathered together to seek solace and fellowship in the face of adversity. The event is non-denominational and non-religious, but it is meaningful and affirming to me that St Martin's has been a sacred place of continuous Christian worship since at least 1222, when there is a first reference to a church on the site, built for the monks of Westminster, surrounded by fields now long gone.

My life changed forever when my husband Chris and I lost our beloved son to suicide on 14 February 2017, two days before his 23rd birthday. At the funeral, the vicar told the vast congregation that it was as though 'Storm Oliver' had suddenly arrived and overwhelmed us all. He said that, in time, the tumultuous seas and hurricane winds would subside and we would see before us a new landscape. Nothing would ever be the same again. He was right.

Our loss was seismic, drawing an indelible line in our lives. We now speak in terms of life before Oliver died and life after he died. Every event and occasion, whether happy, sad or indifferent, is now fixed forever as 'before or after Oliver'.

I also saw the toll it took on others. Oliver's older brother Samuel and our wider family have suffered the trauma and pain of losing someone they loved dearly. His countless friends, too, were just starting out in life with a world full of promise, when they were dealt a heavy hand in losing someone they had grown up with and loved as a brother.

So how do we go on after suffering the deepest of wounds in losing our most precious loved ones to suicide? Each of us will tread our own unique path, for no two people will share the same journey of loss and grief that eventually, we can but hope and pray, will lead to a place of acceptance, even healing.

For me, life beyond suicide means I often mourn the stolen years and decades my son and I would have had together. But I also cherish the memories that bring me so much joy. Losing Oliver has altered me greatly as a person, but I would argue it has been for the good; and both my husband and I believe we are better people today than we were before. My role now, I believe, is to keep my son's spirit alive in this world. I have lit a candle for him, and will guard the flame with all my heart, in recognition of the depth of love we shared.

More importantly, it is because of my son that I have found a deep faith in God and a belief in eternal life. Thus, the title of this book and this chapter has a twofold meaning for me, which I will endeavour to share.

Oliver: A blessing and my teacher

First and foremost, it is a simple, overwhelming need for me, as his mother, to tell Oliver's story, so forgive me for taking this opportunity to write about my son.

From the moment he was born, Oliver brought me happiness. Gazing at him in the hospital cot, I had the sense he was an old soul. Even as a little boy, he was incredibly loving and kind, with a remarkable empathy for others. He was also enormous fun, with an irresistibly infectious chuckle. My memories of him are full of laughter from a baby right up almost until the end of his life, as he never lost that desire to make people happy.

As a pupil at Christ's Hospital School, Horsham, West Sussex, from 11 to 18 years of age, Oliver flourished and did exceptionally well at his studies, gaining four A grades at A level in maths, economics, history and French. He formed deep bonds with school friends. It is a testament to their lasting friendships that some of those young men and women went on to help me form our suicide prevention charity.

Oliver loved to learn and was an avid reader, always with a book in hand, so he was knowledgeable beyond his years, which meant he could mix with people of all ages. After winning a prestigious economics prize in his last year at school, he became involved in the World Traders Livery Company and went to Shanghai on a business trip with members of the Company that same year. Greatly saddened by his passing just four years later, his friends at the World Traders set up an award in Oliver's memory, which is now presented by the Lord Mayor of London every Speech Day at Christ's Hospital School.

His extrovert nature meant Oliver picked up languages easily, learning to speak French, German, Spanish and some Mandarin, so that he could laugh and joke with even more people all round the world. He played sport, particularly tennis, and loved to sing and dance and take part in musicals and plays. He once took the lead role in a jazz show at the Adelphi Theatre and blew us all away that evening. His fabulous and fitting rendition of 'L-O-V-E' is still played today. He was a gifted jazz singer who would have entertained us for years, had he lived.

Like so many young people, Oliver took a gap year after A levels. But he went above and beyond, as usual, by keeping extensive journals of every day of his adventure. He wrote on long-haul flights across continents. He wrote while lying on rickety beds in hostels, under makeshift tents in the Amazon jungle and on interminably long bus rides across Chile, Peru, Bolivia, Paraguay and Argentina. He also wrote on beautiful beaches in Thailand and Australia and on breathtaking mountains in New Zealand.

We found those journals close to where he died in his bedroom at our family home in Worthing, West Sussex, and I felt he had left them there as a gift for us to read. I could hear his voice in every precious line. With the help of friends, I produced a book of his abridged journals called *Oliver's Travels* and filmmakers made a 50-minute documentary called *Olly's Light Travels* in 2024 for when he would have turned 30.

At University College London, Oliver read History, gaining a first-class degree. His dynamism, warmth and charisma meant that he was a 'big name on campus', so the university set up an award in his name – but it wasn't for history. It was for altruism because, probably more than anything else, people remember Oliver for his kindness and compassion and for always putting others first.

Oliver was often seen as a role model to his friends and so many would go to him for help and advice, myself included. He had girlfriends and also friends who were girls, some of whom I am still in touch with.

While no one could resist his outward charms, beneath lay a deeply humanitarian spirit. He was the brightest of stars who continues to shine in our lives, inspiring us to do good.

Oliver died shortly after returning from his third stay in Shanghai, where he was a teacher for the British Council. He made some amazing friends there, two of whom are now trustees of Olly's Future, but for the first time ever he spoke of feeling unsure about the direction his life was taking and expressed a lot of self-doubt. When he returned to England for a month at Christmas, he went further downhill. In early January 2017, he saw a doctor and described feelings of depression and anxiety. An appointment was made for him to see a nurse to have a blood test taken to check his thyroid, which can sometimes affect a person's mood. However, tests proved negative. Shortly after this, Oliver spoke on the telephone to a third clinician, who prescribed him Citalopram and told him to pick up the medication at the in-house pharmacy. It was the first time he'd been prescribed an antidepressant. After just four days of taking the medication, he took his own life. I have no doubt that my son had an adverse reaction to Citalopram.

Working in the field of suicide prevention now and understanding more about the nature of antidepressants, I have discovered there were questions I could have asked, signs I may have missed, and conversations I could have had. But it is pointless feeling guilty and burdened by remorse. I have learned to accept that I did the best I could with the knowledge, experience and understanding I had at the time; and I would urge anyone weighed down by guilt, perhaps even self-loathing, to accept that too.

I know the last thing Oliver would have wanted was to have caused his loving family any pain. I never felt anger towards my son, as some can and do towards those they have lost. How could I, when we loved each other so much? My suffering came in the form of an invisible cloak of sadness, weighing me down for a long time. I had the sense that grief was in every fibre of my being, and was part of the DNA of each and every cell in my body.

My resilience to difficult situations and people is much lower than it was in the past, and for that reason I no longer tolerate things I might once have accepted. My mantra now is to 'only be with people who make me happy and do what makes me happy'. It's simple and effective and is one of the ways my life has been altered for the good, because of Oliver.

There was an outpouring of love when Oliver died. So many people offered help and expressed their sorrow. The house was full of flowers and cards. People would ring the doorbell and leave home-made meals on our doorstep. Our loss revealed the best of humanity.

However, despite the kindness and compassion we received, I felt exposed and vulnerable knowing that our grief was public knowledge, perhaps even the subject of gossip in the town. It was sometimes hard responding to other people's reactions – their shock, concern and on a few occasions their well-meaning but unhelpful comments. I couldn't face going out to the shops, pubs, or cinema in my home town for over two years. I preferred the anonymity of living in London, where I rented some accommodation to be near to my surviving son Samuel when he returned to work there after a break of three months.

The magnitude of 'Storm Oliver' had a far greater impact on my soul than anything else, however. I knew I had been truly blessed in having the gift of Oliver as my son, albeit for such a short time. The overriding feeling was of gratitude for having had such a beautiful soul in my life, who had been the greatest of blessings to me, as well as my teacher.

For Oliver taught me so much about how to live life to the full and to be kind to others. He was a better person than I will ever be.

Above all else, he taught me the most profound lesson of all – that love is greater than anything; it is stronger than death, it endures, grows, it is what makes us human.

God's presence and love

Some people have told me they stopped believing in God and going to church after losing their loved one to suicide. Overwhelmed with despair and a feeling of isolation, there was no way any light could penetrate the darkness and so they lost their faith.

No two people grieve in the same way, but all experiences are equally valid. Couples often respond very differently, despite losing the son or daughter they brought into the world together. So many marriages and relationships break down under the strain of their bereavement, as it is probably one of the hardest things for any person to endure. My husband Chris and I experienced our loss completely differently and we've had to rebuild our life together over the years.

It is our response to those universal truths of love and loss that define us as human beings and it is not until we are faced with these monumental, life-defining moments that we understand ourselves at a profoundly deep level.

Growing up, I went to a school where we said the Lord's Prayer during assembly and sang hymns; however, we never went to church as a family and never talked about Jesus or God. Religious education was a school subject, as far as I was concerned, with very little bearing on my life. Before losing Oliver, I had occasionally attended a local church where I had staged a community play, and I enjoyed going to Christmas carol services. But I would not say I was particularly spiritual.

That changed irrevocably when we lost Oliver. I experienced a sudden and dramatic awareness and understanding of the presence of God in my life. It was almost instant. I now believe this was the second way in which Oliver acted as my teacher. I felt that while my heart was broken, it had broken open to let God's love show me my path and purpose, as well as the life to come, which was revealed through Oliver's dying. *Life beyond suicide*, beyond death – eternal life.

Despite the sorrow, or perhaps because of the sorrow, I experienced a great sense of love and peace. I accepted that Oliver only needed to stay a short while in this world and that his soul had passed on so swiftly to eternal life.

The depth of my grief for him mirrored the depth of my love for him. Through Oliver, I know I am connected to God; and through God, I am connected to Oliver. The two are inseparable.

Perhaps it was the Holy Spirit working in me, or a time of magical thinking – a phrase I have heard too – but for the first two or three years I felt half of me was in this world and half of me in the next. The loss, paradoxically, brought me many blessings and unexplained, almost mystical encounters.

For example, when Oliver died, the person who called the police was someone I had never met before, despite living around the corner from us. The trees were stripped of their leaves, so Jo, a young woman in her 30s, had a distant view of the back of our house and could see what had happened. She was only days away from giving birth to her first child, and had woken early because she was uncomfortable and couldn't sleep.

Just as Oliver was leaving this world, so Jo gave birth to a beautiful baby boy less than a week later. She is a dear friend to me now, and I love her two children (she had another son two years later). I can't help feeling this was Oliver's last gift to me, and another way in which God showed his love and presence.

A little later, Jo told me that something very unusual had happened the night Oliver died. The windows in her front room had blown open. I was staggered. Another sign, perhaps.

The Bible tells us 'God is love' – as plain and as simple as that. I am often reminded of the words of Julian of Norwich, the mystic anchoress who lived in the Middle Ages, who said, 'All shall be well and all shall be well, and all manner of things shall be well.' If I have worries, I try to leave them at the foot of the cross of our Lord Jesus Christ. It is a powerful act of letting go.

The Carmelite monks at Boar's Hill Priory, south of Oxford, have also played a vital role in helping me deepen my relationship with God. My encounter with the priory was seemingly by chance, as a friend and I found out they were running a retreat at the priory when we were looking online for a short holiday. We booked ourselves in for a five-day silent retreat, and I have never looked back since. I have been part of a group of four since 2019 that meets every Monday evening online for silent prayer and to share our insights.

There is a longstanding practice of spiritual autobiography in the Carmelite tradition, with St Teresa of Avila's *The Book of Her Life* and St Thérèse of Lisieux's work *The Story of a Soul* being two examples. Both were Carmelite nuns and two of only four female Doctors of the Church, out of a total of 37 saints, who are said to have made significant contributions to Christian doctrine.

When we understand our own narratives we are better able to be more open to the inflow of the divine. I attended a nine-month 'Living Prayer' course at the priory in 2019. Before starting the course, participants were requested to do a piece of reflective writing – to write their own spiritual autobiography – considering how God had been present or seemingly 'absent' in all the seasons of our life.

It was the first time I had ever reflected on my spiritual journey and those instances or people who had shaped my faith. We were asked to focus on what feeds our soul, what nourishes our spirit and what our soul longs for. It is something I think is useful for everyone to reflect on at some stage in their life.

When I think back over my life with Oliver, there were times I had a sense of precognition about his death, which is very hard to explain. It was as though a greater power or force was at work, creating an unstoppable alignment that resulted in his death. Yet my response has been not to dwell on the sadness, but to harness the love and compassion that has sustained me to do God's will.

The Bible assures us that through prayer and going deeper in faith we will receive 'the peace of God that passes all understanding'.

The 'dark night of the soul', a phrase first used by the sixteenth-century Spanish mystic St John of the Cross, is a very real experience for me, and it was then that the truth was revealed like a diamond against the black.

It was love and compassion that led to our charity – Olly's Future – being formed in 2020. Some of Oliver's dearest friends are the trustees and support me as CEO in our suicide-prevention education work to save further young lives from being lost to suicide. Our motto is 'Love and Light', summing up Oliver's qualities and also all that his loss revealed. We are the future he no longer has on this earth.

Oliver didn't stay long in this world. He passed through quickly, like a shooting star, illuminating the lives of so many and now inspiring us to do good in his memory. I carry him in my heart always and know that through God, we will be reunited one day.

Until then.

A prayer for the suicidal

O Eternal Father, we pray for all those who are suicidal. May your loving hand guide and protect them so they receive the help they need, preventing them from dying from suicide. Let them know that we need them and love them. Show them your love, Lord Jesus. Remind them that they are very special people, filling their minds with beautiful memories.

Give them everything they need so as to ease their pain. Grant that they may find hope, comfort, guidance and healing in every way possible.

Let them feel our love and your love. Carry them when they are weary.

Embrace them and let your love shine down upon them always.

Part Two

3

Losing a Child

CONTRIBUTORS

Shirley Smith

Suicide. Prior to March 2005, it wasn't something I had ever had to give consideration to. A word I possibly came across on the rare occasions I would attempt a crossword. It wasn't something that I knew a lot about. And why should I?

Our lives changed forever on 28 March 2005, when our eldest and much-loved son, Daniel, took his life aged 19. There were no signs, no build-up to that day. He was just a 'normal' 19-year-old. As Dan's mum, I felt responsible for his death; that I had missed so much and should have seen his inward struggle. Struggling to deal with the intensity and complexity of the impact of Dan's death, it hit our family and whole community with the ferocity and fallout of an atom bomb.

The rollercoaster of thoughts in my head churned over and over, revolving from sadness to anger, longing to desperation, and an overwhelming need to know why. Why? Why? Why? I too felt suicidal. And then the pangs of guilt would smash through my head: how could I feel that way, when my other two boys and husband needed me now more than ever? Daniel consumed every minute of every hour of every day. And on the rare occasions I became distracted from these thoughts, I felt guilty for not feeling 'the pain'.

In 2005, shortly after Dan's death, his two brothers, Matthew (10) and Ben (5), along with niece Sarah (12), were supported by a family friend, Suzanne, who was a Samaritan. The children wanted to try to prevent others experiencing a similar loss. They started a campaign to raise awareness of the charity and to encourage people to talk about their feelings, which they gave the name 'If U Care Share'. They truly believed that Dan's death had been preventable. Had he spoken of how he was feeling, the outcome could and would have been different.

In 2010, the If U Care Share Foundation was founded, with three aims: prevention of and intervention into suicide through training, and support for those bereaved by a suicide.

To date, 11,000 young people under the age of 21 have taken part in our Emotional and Mental Health workshops. We truly believe that often people don't want to die, but for seconds they forget how or why they should live. Our message is 'There is always a way.' We now provide training in schools in County Durham and League Football Education and the Premier League in clubs throughout the country.

We have supported 48 people at risk of suicide; we have equipped over 500 adults with emotional and mental health awareness skills; and we launched our suicide prevention and postvention training in May 2015. We have provided practical and emotional support to 380 people touched by suicide and are providing services on behalf of Public Health in our area, working with police to provide support within 48 hours after a suspected suicide. The number of people that IUCSF has supported is now over 10,000, including prevention and postvention and training programmes, and 400 police, including civilian members of police.

We now work alongside other families who are members of a very special group called The Alliance of Suicide Prevention Charities. Most of those involved in TASC have suffered a similar loss, and although we are all different and the relationships we shared with those we lost are unique, we are united in our strength to change the outcome for others; to show that suicide is not inevitable – that it is instead preventable.

Two decades after Dan's death, having worked with hundreds of people touched by suicide, I now know that the myriad feelings, given the enormity of our loss were, and still are, understandable. Time was not a great healer. However, time allowed me to cope differently. Time allowed hope to enter into my life again and whether it was hope that the pain would one day be bearable, or just that I would have hope and nothing else, hope entered back into our lives like a long-lost friend.

Einstein said we should, 'Learn from yesterday, live for today and hope for tomorrow.' We do not want Daniel's life to be defined by the way in which he died but how he lived. He was witty and intelligent with an infectious presence. His manners and strength and warmth for people made him a very popular young man, and his 19 years on this earth were special years. With his love surrounding us I have now learned to live with hope in my heart and hope that we continue our journey united in our determination to make suicide preventable.

Clare Milford Haven

The day after my 21-year-old son James died, on a bleak and cold December evening ten years ago, I went up to his bedroom just to sit, just to smell his familiar smell, and to start the lengthy process of coming to terms with the fact that I would never see my eldest son again. Bizarrely, our family dog was also sitting in his room. She knew something was up, something bad, and she too had gone up there, perhaps to try and make some sense of the whole thing. And we sat there together. Just Purdey and me. It was a very sad and difficult moment for us both.

My other son, Harry, came into James's bedroom. I asked him if he was OK. He said he was OK, but he was worried about me. He said that he was worried that James's death would destroy me. And if it did, it would destroy everything. It was at that moment that I realized what a huge responsibility I had as the mother and mainstay of the family. That I had to keep the show on the road, in particular for my remaining children, Harry and Louisa, but also for my extensive, close family, and dearest friends. Things had to be as *normal* as possible. But I asked myself, how on earth was I going to do this when a child I had given birth to had died and my heart had been shattered into a million pieces?

By chance, I had been given a book by a friend of mine who had also lost a child – Victor Frankl's famous account of his harrowing years as a prisoner of war in Auschwitz, *Man's Search for Meaning*. It was within this book that I found the answer in one short paragraph:

> Forces beyond your control can take away everything you possess, except for one thing, your freedom to choose how you will respond to the situation. You cannot control what happens to you in life, but you can always control what you will feel and do about what happens to you.

'You can always control what you will feel and do about what happens to you.' I turned this sentence over and over in my head. It made sense but how achievable was it when, at the time, everything seemed so out of control and nothing seemed to make sense anymore. James's death was not a part of my life plan. Why had it happened to us? Why, why, why?

It became very apparent very early on that when someone you love dies by suicide, it is a different kind of grief altogether. It is a grief compounded by an overridingly painful emotion, *guilt*. Guilt about the fact that you didn't realize what was about to unfold. Guilt about the fact that you couldn't save someone you love more than life itself in their darkest hour. And you carry this sack of guilt with you everywhere – to bed, when you wake up, to the supermarket, to your office, on holiday, on a lovely walk with the dogs, to your friend's party when someone says something funny and you wonder if it's OK to laugh again ... And it's heavy as hell. So heavy, you feel that it might crush you. And you feel that you may never see the joy in life again because you are so weighed down.

But then gradually, as the days, weeks, months and years pass, the load suddenly starts to become lighter, you stop beating yourself up on a daily basis and you slowly start to feel more 'normal'. You meet other parents and families who are going through a similar process and you begin to feel less isolated, less alone. You start to give back to others. You start to find moments of peace again. You start to feel the joy in life again. You never 'get over it'. You 'get on with it'. And you never 'move on' but you 'move forward' and you start to absorb the intense pain that such a loss brings in its wake, and you begin, very, very slowly, to accept.

And as you accept, you realize that although life as you knew it will never be the same again, like a butterfly emerging from its chrysalis, you come out of the darkness into the light; a little weary, but this time, God has given you wings.

Anna Biggs-Davison

'Loss' is another country, a place none of us wants to be, a place where we end up as part of life's rich cycle. A visit is inevitable; the price we pay for loving.

Patrick took his own life on 6 January 2015, aged 25. He was the eldest of our two adopted sons. He, like his brother, was part of me, my heart, my life and one of the main reasons why I stayed alive. Those boys were my life. If Patrick breathed, I breathed.

He found life difficult, having been a small, premature baby who suffered from endless health problems. He was dyslexic, dyspraxic, impulsive and suffered from a severe form of ADHD. Many months after he died, I discovered that he had also been suffering from an autistic trait, called Pathological Demand Avoidance. While knowing that I was probably the worst possible type of mother to bring up such a vulnerable boy, suffering to a much lesser degree all of my son's disabilities, I loved him passionately. I spent hours just gazing at him in wonder.

'Why are you looking at me?' he'd say. 'Because you are so utterly beautiful,' I would reply. And he was. He was also captivating, exciting, articulate, creative, a free spirit and very much his own man. I couldn't take my eyes off him.

I knew how hard he was going to find life, and he did. Children like him require too much effort, patience, time, understanding. Teachers found him hard to cope with. He was very popular, charismatic and bright, but lacked the ability to concentrate, follow a vocalized train of thought, read at speed, follow a list of instructions or respond immediately to orders. My heart bled for him. So, my grieving for him began early. He had lost who he could be, and he knew it.

I banged on the doors of doctors, health visitors and teachers, but the response was always the same. I won't bore you with the list of negative labels he was given, but they were hard to hear. I felt his agony. He took, quite understandably, refuge in drugs at the age of about 12, with friends who are quite happily walking around today, living normal, fulfilled lives. Patrick had not been born with the same resilience as them. He became an addict. My sense of loss continued. I had lost him to his demons. They were far stronger than him or me.

With his brain becoming increasingly damaged by the drugs he took, he struggled to make each day worthwhile. He read voraciously, wrote essays and poetry, played the piano, enjoyed his friends, from whom he hid the truth of how he was really feeling and the depth of his addiction. We, at home, lived with his demons. A normal life disappeared. We had long ago lost the boy he longed to be: strong, tall, academic, confident and easy-going, like his chosen friends, with the ability to hold down a job. Unfortunately, the only jobs he was qualified to do were mundane, uncreative, repetitive and bored him to distraction; and he could not see the situation changing for him any time soon.

So, he soon understood that the talents he possessed were not required by society: not unless he worked tremendously hard. His ADHD and his drug addiction did not allow that. So finally, one night, he had had enough and ended the pain. I can't say I hadn't seen it coming. I had had a sense, from when he was very young, that he was never going to fit into this world. He was a square peg in a round hole. Patrick was not meant for this world, as his brother put it.

What did loss mean for me? It meant that I wanted to do what any mother does. I wanted to go and find him and bring him home, safe and sound. I searched without ceasing, amid the agony and pain. I looked to my faith, prayer, books, friends, support groups, meditation, mindfulness, yoga and even a shaman and a medium. Surprisingly, they all helped. But finally, I turned to those I loved and those who loved me. And sleep. Blessed sleep. Never have I slept so much. Because of my loss, my life and the person I felt I had been changed for ever, as I knew it had to. I could no longer work full time, hold a sensible conversation even, envisage how a day would pan out, rise from my bed, open a book or, most cruelly, help my younger son and husband to cope with their grief.

What caused the most pain was not being able to do the small things I had always enjoyed doing for my son. I could no longer wash and iron his clothes, shop for his favourite food, watch him playing with the dog, cook for him, hug him, feel him, smell him, hear his voice, argue with him, tell him how precious he was and thank him for making me yet another cup of tea. I have loved deeply and lost a precious part of my very being. I don't blame my son at all. But I do blame the society that he was expected to be part of, egged on by social media, that make-believe tormentor of the 'unsuccessful' ones, the weak, the vulnerable, the lonely. I blame a system that tolerates drugs, and an internet system whereby narcotics can be bought in minutes.

I blame a world that finds no place for those who cannot be moulded a certain way. I fed that boy home-made, puréed organic food, taught him to crawl, walk, sing, read, play, swim, build bonfires, swear, hike through wonderful forests. I mopped his brow when he was ill, planned birthday parties, took nits out his hair, polished his school shoes, kissed him, lay with him when he couldn't get to sleep or had taken yet another drug bought over the internet and imagined that he was a chicken, while lying on a hospital floor. I did everything a mother could, but the demons won.

No one who takes their own life wants to die. They just want the pain to end, and this is the only way that they can see out of the depression and agony in which they are being tormented. I have been asked to meet many young men whose mothers fear they will take the same route as Patrick. I have very little to offer them, because we have not created a world that can support their sons or even hear their voices or admit that they exist. The expectations of society are too high for them even to begin reaching for.

They are wonderful, kind, gentle and good young men who deserve better. What can loss help me to look forward to? I can look forward to the day I too am called away by the Lord, to the day when I can hold my son in my arms again. That will come when the time is right, I know. I just have to be patient and try to make every day remaining to me as calm, peaceful and loving as I can, and offer some comfort to friends who are in the same situation.

I visit Patrick's grave as often as I can, and plant what will grow under a shady tree. I talk to him and say that I love him. It brings some comfort.

Patrick is always with me and I am so very grateful for the 25 years we had together. Enjoy your peace, my son, and know that you are still so very loved. Until then, I will do my best to love and be loved by others, including you.

Niloufar Noorbakhsh

Our son Fabio Ali ended his life on 29 June 2014. He was 23 years old. Fabio was a passionate, vibrant, intensely curious, kind young man. When he smiled you could not help but join him. It was a smile from deep inside that radiated deeply. Fabio was loved by so many people, not just his family; he had friendships with people he had known since primary school and became his extended family. He was not alone.

But that love, my love as his mum, and the love of all those who knew him and were there in his everyday life, was not something he could access on that fatal day, that moment when he could see no other way out of the darkness and despair he was experiencing. It was a life-changing moment for him and subsequently everyone else. His life came to an end brutally and abruptly.

I now view life through a totally different filter – a term I have heard expressed by many people bereaved by suicide. There was their life before the death of their loved one; and their life after that death. As a way of living with such intense, harsh, complicated feelings, I sought out therapy, and it has been helpful. But somehow, I found myself stuck in an everlasting cycle of thoughts and images that became my filter for everyday life. They were there in the small moments: while enjoying the warmth of the sun on my face, a cup of tea, a warm hug, writing an email, anything, everything, my head would chant, 'Fabio's dead.' My body would tighten … I expected this in the big moments; but not in every moment.

The sadness is intense, and the range of emotions complicated and distorted. I know now what is so very common for those of us who have experienced losing a loved one in such a horrific way. I feel it in my body, I hold my breath and tighten inwardly, my muscles stiffen, my stomach retracts, my jaw clamps down and my fingers rub against each other lightly, expressing my nervousness and uncertainty. I am a wild caged lion pacing and roaring the most almighty roar. The roar is ferocious and has no end. I am scared of this lion and what it might do. So I hide that lion, I swallow that roar and choke inwardly.

What I have come to learn is that the body never lies. Everything I am feeling is being expressed clearly by my body. So now I try to listen to it and to take notice. When I catch myself holding my breath, I breathe into that space. If I feel or notice my jaw tighten, I go for a big yawn and feel myself let go just that little bit. I ask the parts of my body what they would say if they could speak. My jaws say they are angry and that they won't let go; my chest says it feels nervous and fearful; my lungs, as they hold my breath back, say it's not safe to be here; my mind keeps me busy with endless questions: it refuses to accept the reality of Fabio's death.

I now acknowledge these parts of my body when I can, for I have come to understand that it is my body's way of keeping me from feeling those deep, dark, big feelings. I was in a perpetual state of fear and disassociation, but I had become so accustomed to feeling this way that it became my norm.

No wonder I was exhausted all the time. The amount of energy being used by my body to protect me was the very thing depleting me. Did I need this kind of protection three years on? What I found out was that often the fear of 'going there' was far more difficult and draining than allowing myself to feel some of those emotions that I thought would envelop and engulf me.

And in those moments where I am able to experience being connected to my feelings, yes, it is often painful and I do feel vulnerable, so very vulnerable. The feeling I now know I have unconsciously and consciously worked so very hard to avoid passes and I am not lost in a black abyss. In that acknowledgement, my body gets to feel it is safe to be present to those feelings. And each time I am able to do that, that message is embedded a little more into my body, allowing those feelings to pass through. And what I'm left connected to is the sadness, and that's OK, because it is so very sad.

I now can allow the lion to be and have compassion for his suffering.

Jenny Dover

I had coffee with a friend recently and we chatted about this and that. Later she sent me a message, 'I just wanted to say that while we were talking, I wanted to mention Aaron.' I was comforted by this – there are few things as lonely as the preoccupation that follows a son's suicide. A preoccupation so powerful that it drives a wedge between oneself and others. But her message brought home to me how hard it is for others to know how, when and what to say.

Not surprising. After all, I too struggle with knowing how much I can say to myself. It's like part of my mind is a guardsman – allowing small manageable excursions into the realms of grief and memory and, of course, into thinking about the moment that my lovely son fell from the building. I tiptoe up to certain images and then flee when it feels unbearable. Like finding the embers of a fire are still scorching hot. At night, the guard is less vigilant – and my mind can feel colonized by terrible imaginings and questions.

I knew a thing or two about loss before my son died – but suicide has a complexity of its own. Guilt may militate against the desire to recover. Washington Irving said,

> The sorrow for the dead is the only sorrow from which we refuse to be divorced. Every other wound we seek to heal, every other affliction to forget; but this wound we consider it a duty to keep open; this affliction we cherish and brood over in solitude.

When someone you love chooses to die it can change you profoundly. Despite my better judgement, I feel invalidated as a mother, and as mental health professional: two defining aspects of myself. Two years on and I feel lost still, finding it hard to recognize the world and my place in it.

It helps to know that I am engaged in a process over which I have only limited control; that the work of mourning and trauma has its own rhythm and will take as long as it needs. I can neither speed it up nor slow it down. I don't need to force myself to look at his last messages or to open my bedside drawer to see his personal effects – phone, wallet, sunglasses…

The poet Emily Dickinson, in her poem 'Tell all the Truth but tell it Slant', wrote about the necessity of facing the truth. But she emphasizes the importance of defending against intolerable pain. She says,

'The Truth must dazzle gradually / Or every man be blind.' In his last phone call to me, Aaron, seeing the world through the distorted lens of severe mental illness, told me that dying was the only solution to his problems. He added urgently, 'You know I love life, don't you, Mum.' This is confirmation that suicide can be a response to a state of mind at the time – and doesn't need to colour the memories of a person prior to that. Aaron lived very intensely and knew joy most of his life. He knew love and loved others. His final email included the words 'I just want my mum.' His love and that of surviving family and friends sustains me.

Finally, I tell myself he is no longer in pain and his suffering has ended. A poem by Gerard Manley Hopkins reflects this.

I have desired to go
Where springs not fail,
To fields where flies no sharp or sided hail
And a few lilies blow.
And I have asked to be
Where no storms come,
Where the green swell is in the havens dumb,
And out of the swing of the sea.

Hamish Elvidge

'My dearest friend, I am going to miss you more than anyone can imagine. Your smile and laugh made me so happy! I am so sorry that you felt you couldn't talk to me. Everything I do reminds me of you. I don't know how I will ever get over this, you were the greatest guy I knew.'

'I will never forget all the good times we had together ...'

'I don't know why you left us ... I only wish you had told someone ... but I think it was in your nature, not to burden anyone else.'

These are the words of some of Matthew's closest friends taken from letters written to Matthew shortly after he took his own life on 20 September 2009.

We had a knock on the door at 2am one Sunday night and two young policemen told us the news. They stayed just a few minutes, and then left. We were on our own from that point onwards. One of the things that has stayed with us from those very early days is a comment made by our vicar. He said, 'You have two things to consider: how you *cope* with your loss, and the fact that there will always be a "Matthew-sized hole" in your family, and things will never be the same; and how you *respond* to your loss: what happens next in your lives.'

A year after Matthew died, his eight closest friends from Newcastle University, who all shared a flat together, cycled 1,000 miles round Great Britain, to each other's houses, ending up at our home on 22 August 2010. They called it 'A thousand miles for Matt'. They wanted to raise funds and 'respond' to their loss. They wanted to make a difference. As a direct result of this, we set up the Matthew Elvidge Trust. As I said in a letter I wrote to Matthew a few months after he died: 'You would be so proud of what the boys have done, as you cared for others and were always there for them. These boys want to make a difference, so that your tragic loss results in something positive: something that prevents others feeling the depth of despair that you were feeling.'

So we have been on a journey ... shaped by Matthew's experience, our family experience and the direct response of his close friends. We have been involved with so, so many people in so many areas related to suicide prevention, bereavement support and education. Together, we persuaded the government to invest in suicide bereavement support in every area of the country. And we are now in the middle of making plans with the health authorities and hope this will make a difference to the lives of thousands of people in the coming years, offering amazing, proactive support to those left behind, just like so many wonderful services do now, but in every area of the country: helping people handle the first thing – the loss, the gap, the devastating impact on parents, siblings, friends and professionals. This is our response to the 'Matthew-sized hole' in our lives.

And then there's education in emotional well-being and mental health: persuading the government to educate our young people on the importance of good mental and emotional health and to invest in providing effective support. The government has, at last, started to recognize this need and made the early stages of response. Physical, mental and emotional health education became mandatory in all schools from September 2020. Universities are now beginning to treat the mental health and well-being of all their students and staff, including suicide prevention, as a real priority.

I often wonder if Matthew, and so many other young people who felt that they had no choice, had been given the opportunity to understand all about mental health – that suicidal feelings are not unusual, how to cope better with difficult periods in life, to talk about feelings and seek help early – whether he would still be with us today.

So thinking about the second thing the vicar mentioned all that time ago – how you respond to your loss – I feel that, with the amazing efforts and collaboration of so many people, and all the different initiatives that we have started – from crisis centres and local suicide bereavement support to zero-suicide ambition, changes to patient confidentiality and consent and primary care education – we have all responded, and are making a real difference to achieve two things: to save the lives of people in the future, so that their families and friends don't experience the same loss; and to ensure that people who are bereaved or affected by suicide receive the support that they need and deserve.

We have all drawn on the love of our family, our friends and each other – as well, perhaps, as the strength of our faith to do this. It has been really tough and we still miss Matthew every day. But maybe, just maybe, it will change the outcome for someone else; for another family.

Here are some words sent to us shortly after Matthew died.

It is hard to feel serene when our world is not complete ... when one who once brought wholeness to our lives has gone. Yet, in the emptiness their passing leaves behind, we are not alone. For we have the companionship of the living ... and even our loved ones who have died still live in our hearts ... for what they were is part of what we are. We honour them best when we live, as they would wish ... fully and happily ... even in the shadow of our loss ... and so draw closer to the source of life, in whom every life finds meaning ... purpose ... and hope.

Angela Forster

I'm Sasha's mum. Being Sasha's mum shouldn't be the thing that defines me, because I am so many other things too – I'm Perdi's mum, a wife, a daughter. But it's being Sasha's mum that has had the greatest impact on me, and who I am. Sasha was 'well known' to services, dying age just 20, while an inpatient on a mental health unit. No one, not the police, the hospitals, nor her Community Mental Health team were surprised when she died. But I was. I thought the strength of my love would be enough to keep her alive. It wasn't.

Sasha was on the autistic spectrum and had OCD. A combination of events sent her OCD spiralling out of control. I was faced with an alien world of child and adolescent mental health services, sectioning and inpatient wards. I felt relegated to the background as professionals took over responsibility for my daughter, especially as they always referred to me as 'mum'. 'Are you mum?' they asked. At 18, when Sasha was transferred from child to adult mental health services, there followed two years of hell. I say hell, but nothing compares to the hell of continuing to live when your child is dead. But still, it was pretty grim. I lost count of the number of times Sasha went missing, overdosed, or was sectioned. I went from someone who liked a comfortable eight hours sleep a night to someone who could function with no sleep at all. The telephone numbers of friends were gradually replaced by those of local police forces, mental health services and hospitals. Instead of packing to go away for holidays, I had my hospital rucksack packed and ready by the front door. It contained everything I needed to spend days and nights in A&E with Sasha.

Sasha didn't want anyone to know how ill she was, so I became adept at deceit. The 21-hour treatment for an overdose became a 'girls' weekend away' when I was really spending the night on the floor next to Sasha's hospital bed. I became an expert on her illness, and wouldn't hesitate to argue with professionals who didn't have the same depth of knowledge and experience. I knew the Capacity Act and the Mental Health Act. I could fight Sasha's corner. I became feisty and strong. But as we hurtled from one crisis to the next, I had neither the time nor the energy to feel. I shut down emotionally to cope with the traumatic situations I was dealing with on a daily basis. I no longer panicked at the possibility of Sasha overdosing. Things that would have freaked me out years ago, like self-harm, were now commonplace.

It wasn't all bad though. I longed for the comfort of a bed; but sitting on the floor outside her room, night after night on suicide watch, meant I spent many hours talking with Sasha. It gave me the opportunity to repair our relationship, which had been damaged when she was placed in a unit 80 miles from home. It also gave us the chance to have those difficult conversations. Talking openly and honestly, about the unmentionable, I spent hours and hours trying to persuade Sasha not to choose death over life. I learned to live with impotence of knowing that your child intends to die, but not being able to stop her. I didn't have to ask why she felt the way that she did. I knew why. When she wouldn't be swayed, we spoke about her ideas for her funeral, what she wanted to wear, her choice of music. These experiences all added layers to me, to who I was. They taught me empathy, patience, and made me less judgemental. They altered me, but it was losing my baby girl to suicide that broke me.

Her death changed everything: shattered the very essence of me. When I started putting it back together, there were just too many pieces. Some pieces are the same. But others have gone forever. My life continues to be a battle, not with the noisy turbulence of psychiatrists and police, hospitals and units, but in the silence of each morning, the long days and the quiet nights. The battle to continue to live.

As I negotiate my way through the new landscape of my life, balancing grief in one hand and life in the other, I'm learning how to handle the emotions that drain me – the pain, the rage, the exhaustion. No one warns you just how exhausting grief can be. Sasha no longer stands right in front of me, blocking all else from view. She now walks beside me, each and every day. I will always carry the weight of her with me. Because I am Sasha's mum.

Sangeeta Mahajan

Four hundred and ninety-nine days.

That's how long it's been since our son Saagar left us. He was 20 years old. Apparently, he left by choice. What sort of choice? I don't know. I never will. How did he get to that point? How did we get through all these days and months without him? I have no clue. Life has been cleaved mercilessly into 'before' and 'after'. How can this unthinkable, unimaginable happening be for real? That gorgeous, naughty smile, that kind and generous heart – how can it just disappear?

The mind constantly goes back to 'before' and rearranges events in order to eliminate the 'after'. But we are here in the 'after', which feels like a tiny cage of barbed wire. Sitting here rudderless and alone, I am lost. I am not alone in the sense of being without people who love me, but I am the only person who is his mother. I am lost without him. None of this makes any sense. This is not how it is supposed to be. It is not in the script.

Now what? His drum kit, cricket bat, books, T-shirts, shorts and trainers are still here. I am still here. In a way, he is here. In our smiles and tears. In the hearts of all those who love him. Love. Although my mind has doubted it, my heart knows it to be pure and eternal. Like a river that starts as a glacier and ends as the ocean, love changes and flows.

When I want to see Saagar, I close my eyes and be with our love. The light of love comes through the barbed wire cage. In this light I can see the grief, guilt and anger as nothing but distortions of love. Just like white light is not a colour but the sum of all possible colours, love encompasses everything. If there were no love, there would be no sorrow. They are reflections of each other. While engulfed in darkness, I see the light of love and hang on to it. It is my anchor in this choppy sea. I can depend on it. Like a night traveller navigating her way through the dark, love is my north star. I can trust it to always find me. It is the light of love that has got us through the past 499 days.

As Rumi says, 'The wound is the place where the light enters you.'

Sharon Grenham-Thompson

It was an ordinary Friday afternoon, 3 September 2021. I was busy in the kitchen, preparing for a family visit: the first since we'd moved into our new house. As I buzzed around, humming to myself, drinking my morning coffee, I had no idea that by teatime my world would be shattered. My 17-year-old son Leo took his life just before 2pm – the police were at my door at 4pm. On that terrible day I lost a son, my other children lost a brother, my husband a stepson. Leo was also a grandchild, a godchild, a cousin, a nephew, a pupil, a teammate, a friend. The waves caused by his suicide fanned outward like a tsunami in the days that followed the news, encompassing not only those who knew him, but also those professionals who, in various ways, had to deal with the aftermath. Even our cat and dog were left confused and anxious.

We've had the nightmare of investigations, an inquest, lawyers and police and insensitive bureaucracy. We've had to face what would have been his 18th birthday, and the day he should have received his A level results. There have been the public holidays, the private anniversaries, the silly little everyday reminders that trip you up when you're least expecting it. Oh, the agony of his shoes in the cupboard, his coat on the hook, his favourite food on the supermarket shelf! Much of it seemed unreal – it still does – and no matter how many memorial plaques I fix, trees I plant and visits to his grave I make, there's a large part of me that still hasn't grasped that he's not going to walk back through the door one day.

In fact, there's a large part of me that feels ... unmade. Dislocated, dissolved. Scattered into pieces, blown to the four winds, like litter on the side of the road. I don't know how to gather myself in again. I've had to grapple with devastating guilt, endless questions, utter bewilderment. The most devastating and unanswerable question in the world – why? There's been horror, anger, fear, and a sense of loss that at times I've only been able to express in screams or the wordless sounds of deep, deep keening. The earth has seemed out of kilter, and I've lived outside of time. Future doors have been slammed shut, present moments are altered profoundly, and even my sense of the past, and what was true and reliable and real, has been rocked to the core. The pain has been physical, emotional, mental, spiritual. I'm not really sure how I survived the first 12 months. In fact, there were times when I didn't think I would – or should.

But here I am. Here I am knowing that I'm not alone. That seems to me both utterly tragic and strangely comforting. That there are others who are walking a similar path. There's no doubt that the unfailing support of my husband, the love of my family and friends, the forbearance of my colleagues, and the kindness of complete strangers has helped me to hold on. It seems to me in this, the worst of human experiences, that while we may feel powerless, we can hold a light for one another when the way ahead seems dark. And I hope we can hold a light for those who are in such a lost place themselves that they feel they cannot stay.

When you lose someone to suicide, all their potential seems to disappear. At least, that's how I saw it at first. Now I sense I have inherited Leo's life – his potential, his character, his gentle soul. I will guard it and cherish it, carry it within me as I did when I carried him before he was born. And I will look for its reflection in the faces of those I meet, loving them as I have loved him.

Mike McCarthy

The fragrance of a rose induces a sense of nostalgia for me of happier days and childhood – whether carried as a buttonhole on my schoolboy blazer for a family wedding, or drawing me in with scent into Grandma's garden. The roses represented light, security and innocence. Where have the roses gone?

I look back to 20 February 2021 and wonder what I must have been thinking as I went to bed and closed my eyes. Did I give thanks for the good fortune that life had granted me? Did I give a thought to the blessings of a wonderful family and a good home? In all honesty, I can't remember. But I do remember the call at just after 3am from my son's fiancée. And I do vaguely remember the two-hour drive to their home through a grim, wet, February night. And when we arrived, I remember seeing a pair of old shoes on the lawn that had been used by my son Ross just two days earlier to dress a snowman for his three-year-old son Charlie. The snowman had melted, and all that was left were the shoes. On a day such as that, the scene spoke of unbearable loss and the fragility of life.

But inside the house Ross had left a letter full of loving farewells to his family and urging Charlie to be brave. The police took it away but when, after some pleading, we eventually got it back, Ross spoke to me for one last time. His words went straight to my heart. Among the living words he said: 'Please fight for mental health. The support is just not there.' After ten years of suffering with depression, my son had asked for therapy, been put on a six-month waiting list – and died two weeks into the wait. As he faced his last moments, he recognized a cause to be championed in a world of which he knew he would not be a part. 'Please fight for mental health. The support is just not there.'

I now think of the immediate aftermath of his death as my driftwood days, when I lost all direction and hope. I filled the void by trying to find any scrap of solace; I stroked the leaves of a tree planted in our garden to celebrate Ross's birth. I went to throw a rose in his favourite colour into the Derbyshire river where he swam as a boy and as a teenager; and I watched as the yellow flower floated to who knows where.

It's been hard to process the memories of the son we adored. It remains a battle to think clearly about the good times, because the guilt emerges even though I try hard not to beat myself up – reminding myself that we loved each other, and that I would give anything to see him again, if just for one hour. Had I always said the right thing? Had we talked enough? Did I do all the things that a dad is supposed to do for his son?

What I do know is that my heart still bursts with pride when I think of the stocky and lovable, live-wire little boy, the unsure teenager who worked his way through academic struggles to become an industrial electrician with a workhorse mentality. How at home he would create a playtime obstacle course with cushions, blankets and chairs for his beloved son Charlie. How his flinty, crazy humour would fill us with laughter and love. How he would sway to the rhythm of a ballad with Charlie in his arms, or sit on the floor during Charlie's bathtime and talk to him endlessly even when his baby son was young enough to respond only in gurgles. How he would instinctively stand up for life's underdogs and see the humanity first in every incident, discussion or debate. I am overwhelmed with regret that the chance to help him has gone.

But in the fog following his death, Ross kept whispering the words: 'Please fight for mental health.' And in the grief, the words began to give me direction. In every sport, we celebrate physical prowess with an incalculable number of symbols – trophies, medals and so on. But where were the symbols for mental well-being? At the very heart of our society, where were the conversations about the something that robs us of so much promise, potential and hope?

In 2023, the Baton of Hope – so beautifully designed and created by Thomas Lyte, goldsmiths and silversmiths to the royal family – was carried through twelve cities in twelve days, prompting discussions and connections long overdue. In one year, we created a Workplace Charter, encouraging employers to play their part in a more compassionate society. We helped establish new groups and much greater interest in a subject that for generations has been overlooked or even ignored. Almost a thousand baton bearers walked through the streets in what was endorsed by the prime minister as the biggest suicide-prevention initiative the nation has ever seen. But our journey has just begun.

Different people see different things in the Baton of Hope. Some see an upward spiral leading to a swirl of semi-colons representing the belief that, with positive action, we can create a future for those who are at risk of losing hope. Inside the darkness of the handle are inscribed the words of Desmond Tutu: 'Hope is being able to see that there is light despite all of the darkness.' To me the baton represents an unfolding flower. A symbol of love and compassion. A new golden rose. Fresh hope.

Mike Palmer MBE

Beth was just 17 when she died by suicide. The world lay at her feet. She had a wonderful life to live, full of singing, dancing and laughter. What happened to my happy little girl with all her dreams and ambitions? I will never know; unless I see her on the other side, that is.

She was there one minute, then gone the next. I was shattered in an instant of realization that she could not be saved. I thought I had done a pretty good job, as a father, of equipping her for life. But I had not thought to protect her from her own mental health. I had failed and wanted to die with her. The world changed into a colourless, alien landscape. Everything that should have been familiar was different. Family and friends were unrecognizable and unreachable. Time seemed to stand still in a silent scream of agony. How could this horror happen to my family? Suicide only happened to other people.

I was desperate and I knew it. But some sort of self-preservation kicked in. I shunned alcohol in the knowledge that it would cloud my mind and lead to certain death: a contrary decision, as I was certainly suicidal, and with great clarity had made plans to take my own life. All the early stages of grief were playing out. Denial, anger, bargaining and depression. This was truly a world of darkness. But as time moved on, as it always will, I began to see a few chinks of light. Rather than hold my feelings in, as maybe a stereotypical man would, I needed to talk and learn about what had made Beth do something so terrible. My time was filled with courses on mental health, suicide prevention and hours of research on what happens when you die. Is the end of life a black hole or is there something beyond? My spiritual beliefs now bring me some comfort.

In the early days, friends and relatives bore the brunt of my nocturnal rantings. Then new people started to come into my life. They had experience in all aspects of suicide. Maybe not intentionally, but somehow I was reaching out. These individuals often remained faceless due to Covid, but understood my pain and could empathize with the visceral emotions of heartbreak that were now part of my very being. They all played a huge part in saving my life. Finding a purpose to carry on became clearer, and gradually I started to refocus. My beloved family needed me. I was learning to carry my grief, but seeing them bent double with theirs was unbearable. I could not make things worse by taking my own life. My philosophy was now, 'I will die one day, so why not put up a fight in the meantime.'

Indeed, I wanted to pick a fight, and the cause was there in front of me – to prevent young suicide, and stop other families going through this immeasurable pain. It sounds noble, but I needed this challenge as much as it needed me. Three Dads Walking, with Andy and Tim, truly came at the right time.

Survival is now the name of the game. Other bereaved parents will, I am sure, resonate. I have put up defences to protect myself from the memories of my little Beth, who I love so much. I will never revisit family holiday pictures of Majorca, Mexico or Disney. It is almost as if thinking of those happy times will destroy me. Life now has purpose; I have jobs to do. Yet I still feel empty and incomplete. I suppose I always will. Gone is the strong firefighting dad I was before. Deep sadness is very much part of my world – even though I find myself laughing from time to time; and surely I can be forgiven for that.

Indeed, why would I not be sad? My youngest daughter Beth died by suicide. And I miss her, so much.

Thelma Ridgway

I'm the mother of two amazing children: one I hold in my arms, the other I hold in my heart. My husband Ian and I always feel that Penny Grace Lois Ridgway, our daughter and first born, now 25, is the quintessential English rose. We adore her. Our second child, Lee Jason Shaun Ridgway, our beautiful millennium boy, joined us in 2000. He was born on our wedding anniversary, which thrilled us. He radiated joy and became known at home as Sunshine. He was absolutely brilliant.

As he grew, he lived life to the max, showing such will and determination. A force of nature, excelling in all aspects – kind, sensitive and popular. We were awed by his sheer enthusiasm. We still are. How he illuminated the day of everyone he encountered, such fun, so caring, our shining supernova, truly a star. A beacon exuding love and laughter with a gorgeous cheeky smile. We felt he did everything bigger, brighter, harder, faster – and he did. We cherished him.

Sadly, everything changed when Lee, aged just 16, tragically ended his life. We were devastated. We had no idea he was struggling: he hid it so well. The light that had completed our family had faded. And so did we. Several years on, I've learned so much about heartbreak and how to navigate it. With lots of support and the passing of many seasons, those terrifyingly dark days, when we battled the storms of anguish, slowly subsided and the sun began to flicker and shine again. Penny named a star for her brother in the Auriga constellation. We set up two causes in his honour – Lee's Sunshine Fund, raising money for Papyrus Prevention of Young Suicide, and Lee's Sunshine Legacy, an advocacy offering hope to other families seeking support.

The main thing I've learned, though, is that Lee hasn't really left: because energy never dies. I feel his presence and aura in the everlasting force and golden glow of the sun. He's always there, omnipresent behind the clouds, iridescent in emerging rainbows and beaming brightly when the rays majestically break through. It's wondrously soothing and gloriously healing. Though still missing him desperately and loving him endlessly, we know our aptly named sunshine boy Lee truly is the light that nurtures our precious rose. Penny is now thriving – blooming again; and so are we.

I hope our story offers some comfort, that love and light are indeed eternal. If you sometimes feel those elements are elusive, just wait awhile, let their luminescence find you – because they will. There can be brighter times ahead.

I've found great comfort in the Sing Their Name choir. The choir formed under the compassionate and encouraging guidance of Adele Owen and Dan McDwyer. We hope our singing brings hope to others. We would love to see more Sing Their Name choirs form around the country as we know just how beneficial it's been to our own unique and differing journeys. As a group of suicide-bereaved people from Greater Manchester, we find solace, connection, friendship, healing and hope through singing. Together we pay tribute to our lost loved ones through songs that poignantly resonate but also uplift us. We think of each of them, our sons, daughters, mothers, fathers, brothers, sisters, partners, so many family members and dear friends, now and forever. We wear our badges with the treasured faces of our loved ones on our choir T-shirts close to our hearts as we continue to sing proudly in their names.

Singing is very therapeutic, but we're more than just a choir. We're also a band of grief warriors who have made close bonds that remain long after the words have been sung. We form a vital peer-support network where we collectively weather the tide of loss as it ebbs and flows. When tears fall like pouring rain, we take shelter together under that protective umbrella of joint understanding. There's laughter too, lots of it, among the sunny smiles and warm hugs. Our unity is awesome. It helps to know we're not alone.

Believe me: you are not alone.

4

Losing a Loved One

CONTRIBUTORS

Angela Samata

How easily my mind slips back to that time. In the early days after you'd gone, we pulled together and tried to navigate our way through the strange, new, misty land that we found ourselves unexpectedly inhabiting. It was a world of little sleep and many, many unanswered questions. Those early days of numbness, of shock; days of wondering where you were, half-expecting you to walk through the door, wondering why everyone had descended on our house, the living room, crammed with faces from our past and long, restless nights of wishing that the morning would bring an end to this worst of nightmares.

The early days of painful phone calls, breaking the news to unsuspecting family and friends – their voices lifting as they heard mine, then dropping as my tone revealed the terrible message I had to deliver. I spent the remainder of most of those calls managing their grief and reassuring them, and then falling apart a little after the receiver went down. The early days when I held our children as they cried for you, I wondered if my tears would ever come, and once they did, I wondered if they would ever stop. Our babies have grown since those early days into handsome, towering men, but it was in the valley of my grief that my mind turned to them and the legacy of your parting; a legacy that stays with me even today.

The early days when I discovered the kindness of strangers and friends and my previously unknown ability to drink vast quantities of tea while surviving on a diet of toast. The early days when it felt like you belonged to everyone else – to people in suits and uniforms who'd never heard your voice or witnessed your beautiful smile. In the early days I'd often catch a glimpse of you, just the side of your profile as I went about my daily business. My heart would quicken as I saw you just turn a corner ahead of me. But, of course it wasn't you. It was my wishful thinking.

As the shock of the early days turned into the slow, painful realization that I'd never speak to my lover again, so the pain in my chest lowered into my stomach and stayed there until those early days turned into years. And, although I could feel a change, the end of the early days, I still couldn't be the last person to close *our* front door.

Amy Meadows

I became bereaved by suicide on the most glorious of English summer days on 1 June 2009 when my beautiful, wise, compassionate and much adored mum took her own life at the age of 61. That day my family's lives were turned upside down, inside out, back to front as we had to all start the long, difficult path of reimagining our futures without her as our guiding hand, our shining light – especially my father, with whom she had shared her life for almost 45 years.

I never expected at 35 to have to deal with the death of a parent. And it would have been inconceivable to me back then that I would have someone I know and love die by suicide. I know now, though, how naive that was: suicide can strike anyone – male, female, young and old, rich and poor. It is an indiscriminate visitor to 6,300 households across the UK each year. It arrives uninvited to steal lives and put those of the loved ones into turmoil.

A death by suicide brings with it a unique form of bereavement. A loss that painfully stabs away at you with its incessant asking of unanswerable 'whys' and the very many 'what ifs'. A loss that envelopes you because of the relentless guilt from feeling you didn't do enough and that you could have changed the outcome. A loss that confounds and confuses as it invariably goes against the natural timing and method of how death most usually happens. Suicide tortures your mind in other ways too – at least, it did for me. I found myself developing an obsessive focus on what it would have been like to have been my mum in her final weeks, days, hours. Like a forensic scientist, I imagined the minutest detail. This included replaying how she came to her choice of method of death, and whether she would have felt any pain, or if she had last-minute regrets, too late, about the path she had set in motion.

For me, the most difficult manifestation of my grief was, by far, losing any ability to recall my mum's unique presence day-to-day. To picture her being and doing all the things with, for and around me, for all those years. In my mind, the simple word 'mum' became totally and inextricably linked to the word 'dead'. I was no longer able to recall her alive – to see her loving face, to hear her gentle voice, to feel the stroke of her velvety hands, to bask in her warmth. I couldn't remember returning to the gentle comforts of my family home after school, or enjoying a cup of tea together as adults, her playing with my young children, or her steady advice given out during our regular calls. I grasped at the very few recollections I had – but they seemed like one-dimensional memories, mainly prompted by the family photos that adorn the walls of my home. I felt I was clawing desperately for scraps to try and reconnect me to my past life with her.

Others have told me how they have had the same experience. Maybe the loss of memories is something that happens to protect us when we are in the depths of our grief. A sort of lockdown mechanism to encourage us to focus on surviving the physical manifestations of grief that strike so hard in the early days: the sleeplessness, lack of appetite, the sense of a dark, heavy, malignant force deep in your stomach. Maybe so, and maybe Mother Nature knows best, but I found it one of the most distressing and debilitating aspects of my bereavement.

At the very time I most wanted, and felt I needed, to recall my mum, she was gone. Like a will-o'-the-wisp, I could barely make out her form. On rare occasions, she came all too fleetingly into my dreams and I would wake in the morning with a profound sense of joy at having seen her again. I would desperately try to hold on to these glimpses but within just a few minutes they would ebb away and then vanish completely. I feared I would be trapped forever in this alternative reality, this deep valley, where I knew I had had a mum – my very existence was testimony to that, as were the important values and outlooks that she has instilled in me – but yet, I would have no ability to recall her being in my life. I found it very scary and very lonely.

But, like the snowdrops or daffodils that break through the frosty grass, taking no heed of the heavy grey skies and frosty temperatures, I have now passed through the winter of my grief. Slowly, slowly, my images and memories of my mum are starting to bloom. It has been a gradual process, but increasingly I sense her – I can feel, see and hear her. And it is bringing colour and vitality to my life, just like she did when she was alive. It means I now hold my mum close to me as a real, living person – and can be reminded of the times we shared; our lives entwined.

I am who I am because of my mum. If my profound grief is what I have had to suffer as recompense for having her in my life, then I would go through this again and again. So even having had to face the horror of her loss, I give thanks each day for having had every precious moment together.

Before she died, my mum left a simple, but immensely powerful gift, and it is a gift that I want to share with you all. She left this short note: 'Please everyone, remember me with a smile.' She wanted all to recall her with her beautiful, gentle smile on her face. Not a sad, stricken face on the dark days that proceeded her death, or in her dying moments. She wanted to be remembered happy and alive. But she also wanted ME to smile as I remembered her. To recall my memories with my face upturned. And it is this which has given me the strength and determination to make the most of the gift of life that she gave to me. For that, I will be entirely grateful for her, for she has shown me how to choose to live. I haven't and can't always control what happens in my life. But I can choose how I feel and how I respond. And my choice is with a smile. I hope that way I can bring as much joy to others as my mum did to all those who knew her.

I hope too that you can remember your loved ones with a smile.

Sharon McDonnell

Like most people, suicide and its implications were not on my radar, until my brother's death. However, if I had ever considered this issue, I would have thought that it only happened to other people and their families. Sadly, I have learned from personal experience that this is not the case. My brother died by suicide on 29 December 1990. He was 29 years of age and left a wife aged 27, a daughter aged 8, a mother, father, one brother and four sisters ranging in age from 12 to 30. I was the eldest.

He had never been diagnosed as clinically depressed nor mentally ill. Neither had he made any previous attempts, nor shown any overt signs of severe depression. There was no indication of his impending death. My brother's death has had a profound effect upon my family – each of us attempting to cope with his loss in our own way. My own experience taught me that the relationship between mother and child, father and child, and between siblings differ in many ways. Therefore, even though family members have all lost the same person, their feelings of grief and sense of loss are quite different. Each member of my family experienced an array of emotions, such as denial, shame, shock, anger, distress and self-blame.

I was deeply distressed to think that my brother, who had seemed so well-balanced and in control of his own life, had felt that he had no option other than to die. For many months I tormented myself by worrying and wondering how he had felt as he planned his own destruction. Was he crying? Was he angry? And I also questioned why he felt that his only option was to die. Consequently, the question 'Why?' dominated my thoughts for a long period; principally, why had he felt that he couldn't speak to anyone about his distress? The loss of my brother had a profound effect on my assumptive world and that of my family. I also questioned other aspects of life: if we couldn't predict my brother's death, what other disasters were in store for us? What other fate awaited us? Would another family member die as a result of self-destruction? Was suicide hereditary? Thus I realized that for many in the early stages of suicide bereavement, the world becomes an unpredictable and frightening place.

As time has passed, I have worked through my grief. I no longer torment myself about why my brother chose to end his life. I have learned that this is a fruitless quest and I have learned to accept what I cannot change. However, I do believe that nobody can possibly understand how it feels to be bereaved through suicide unless they have experienced it themselves. Therefore, if an adequate and appropriate support service is ever to be provided, it is necessary for those bereaved by suicide to find the courage to share their painful thoughts and experiences to enable professionals to acquire a clearer understanding of the emotional pain suffered by those bereaved by suicide. I am encouraged and humbled that the service at St Martin-in-the-Fields for those affected by suicide welcomes anyone who is affected by suicide, ranging from those who are feeling suicidal, those who have made a suicide attempt, those bereaved by suicide and professionals who come into contact with this vulnerable population. While I am mindful of the intense loss and pain experienced by most people involved in the service, I am inspired by the courage, empathy and sensitivity of everyone involved. We witness it in so many ways. During this special service, we listen but don't judge, we reach out to others, even when many of us are struggling to cope ourselves. Such responses give me faith in humanity and reveal the level of resilience and compassion among those affected by suicide.

It has been many years since my brother died. At the time there was no emotional compass for our loss. All we had was each other. No family to compare with or provision of support. I have seen dramatic changes since my brother's death and include the following. We now have the

Survivors of Bereavement by Suicide (SOBS) self-help groups. We have the Support After Suicide Partnership, which includes 25 organizations committed to improving the care that those bereaved by suicide receive. Suicide prevention is now a key priority for the NHS and the government. One of the key objectives of the Suicide Prevention Strategy in 2012 is to provide better information and support to those bereaved or affected by suicide. Public Health England and the National Suicide Prevention Alliance have recently developed key documents on how to develop suicide bereavement services locally. Self-harm is now a key priority in the Revised Suicide Prevention Strategy. More attention is being paid to children who are deemed at risk of dying by suicide. And evidence-based suicide bereavement training now guides health professionals on how to care for those bereaved by suicide.

I am mindful that those affected by suicide have had mixed experiences in relation to the care that they have received. We all should receive timely and appropriate support, whether we are feeling suicidal, have made a suicide attempt, or are bereaved by suicide.

I am determined that something positive and meaningful will come from my brother's death. As a direct result, all that I do in this field is in memory of my brother Alexander McDonnell. We all can make a difference in memory of those we have loved and lost. Coming together, having a united voice and being prepared to share our vulnerabilities are powerful reminders that together we can make a difference.

David Robb

On a sunny summer's morning in July 2013 my beloved wife of 35 years left our home wearing her wedding ring but no other jewellery; walked to Fulham Broadway underground station and ended her life beneath the wheels of a city-bound District Line tube. There ... I said it. I wouldn't have been able to do that without breaking down until recently. That's what the passage of time does.

It doesn't heal – I believe the saying that 'time heals' is a lazy cliché – but somehow one gets used to the peculiar new reality, whether one wants to or not – and at the beginning, believe me, I didn't want to. Another lazy cliché is the one which says, 'That which doesn't kill you makes you stronger.' No. I am irrevocably weakened and diminished by my wife's suicide – perpetually bewildered that our deeply cherished love could be swept away in an instant. The disconnect between what one understands and what one comprehends remains.

I understand that my Briony was severely mentally disturbed when she took her life – possessed by anorexia nervosa – but I cannot comprehend how she was able to embrace violent oblivion rather than a long, loving life with me. I couldn't have loved any human being more. But it wasn't enough to keep her alive. I used to believe that shock was a short-lived emotion – another cliché. It isn't. I will go to my grave shocked.

My personal view is that the suicidal state comes to the person, not the other way around. I believe it presents as an intimate friend, a confidante, and – significantly – it offers a conclusion, an end to the private misery and the public chaos. Thus it becomes the dominant element in any retrospective assessment, far more potent and influential than family and friends who don't understand anyway and would surely be altogether better off without this troublesome failure. This is what all of us bereaved by suicide have to try, somehow, to accommodate: that our loved ones who have taken themselves away from us were in an altered state, and in that state, they chose a conclusion over us.

How, then, does life recover? It happens because that's what the passage of time does. It happens irregularly, in fits and starts. It's not gradual. It's not linear. There are times when it ceases to happen, and the horror returns. But one morning, unbidden, a day dawns when you find yourself enjoying something – the weather, the company of friends, a weekend away, a sporting event, perhaps something unexpected. A new life glimpsed. Not the same – not as complete, not as innocent – but a life that is worth living. I still think of Briony every day, but I no longer think of her every second of the day. This, then, is where I've arrived: still in a state of flux, but able to appreciate life again – most of the time.

In the inspiring and calming words of E. M. Forster, 'We must be willing to let go of the life we have planned, so as to have the life that is waiting for us.'

Alison Jordan

I tell the story of my 24-year-old brother's suicide regularly. Five years after his death I set up a charity in his name that supports others experiencing suicide bereavement. People are often interested in how the charity began. I have developed a well-rehearsed speech and set of answers to questions I am used to reciting. I have got to the stage where

I am able to do this with a smile to avoid invoking tricky feelings in those that I am speaking to. I have never deviated from that script. Until now.

As I recall the early days following Pete's death, I remember and feel the confusion and fear of when he was reported missing, I remember and feel the frustration and determination to find him alive and well that fuelled me over the next five days. I remember and feel the sensation of a physical punch to my stomach when the police lady told me he had been found dead. I remember and feel the immediate need to be strong for everyone else, my family and my children, to take control of and attend to the formalities: a contradictory feeling which didn't permit me to attend to my own grief, which rested heavily on my shoulders. I remember and feel the overwhelming urge to 'investigate' the circumstances of his death, his final hours, interrogating his phone, his friends, his laptop, searching his bedroom – so desperate was I to fathom the unfathomable. I remember and feel the exhaustion that overtook me the day after the funeral, with nothing left to do – how my grief stripped me of my energy, leaving me unable to go to work. I remember feeling unsafe in the world, constantly scanning everyone dear to me for the slightest sign they were having thoughts of taking their own life. I remember fixating on the sound of his laughter, worrying incessantly that I would forget. I remember frantically searching my wedding album for photos of him and being distressed as I realized there was not one. I took this as a sign that I was the most terrible big sister and it was all my fault, thinking that had I been a better one he would still be here. In the early days those thoughts and emotions would ride on waves that would knock me off my feet. It seemed that each time I got up another would come and knock me down all over again.

Strangely, I also remember that spring as being the most colourful I have ever seen, in contrast to the darkness inside of me. Daffodils seemed more yellow, and the fresh leaves seemed greener. I noticed clouds and how pretty they looked against a vibrant blue sky. When my energy returned, it was in abundance; there was a feeling in me I hadn't ever experienced, I had a strong sense that something positive was going to happen or change but I had no idea what. People say suicide bereavement is grief with the volume turned up. I would say that for me, everything in my life, both positive and negative, was turned up.

As I reflect, allow and acknowledge these feelings and memories, and mull them over, it's clear that this wave isn't going to knock me off my feet. It makes me sad, it makes me cry and it makes me very tired as I write this: but I have also been able to go to work and do my job, even hold a session of grief recovery for a group of suicide-bereaved mums.

I may not fully visit my grief very often, but I think about Pete every day. Sometimes just a fleeting thought when I catch a picture of him on the Pete's Dragons website, or sometimes a full memory of something he said or did. But mostly it is to gently berate him when I am overwhelmed at work or having to dress in a giant fluffy orange dragon suit and entertain children. Then I imagine him laughing – because I have never forgotten that laugh.

I now know that I don't need to be scared of visiting my grief, and although I can feel the feelings associated with it if I choose, nowadays it is just that – a choice. In the early days I had no choices, I was on a rollercoaster and there was no getting off. My grief remains as it was and always will. The wave is smaller and gentler. I can choose whether I visit it or not – but it lives inside of me, because of my love for the person I lost.

It seems to me that the love that we give and receive is what gets us into this mess in the first place. So it must be that very same love that gets us back out.

Amandip Sidhu

I am bereaved by suicide. My older brother died in November 2018. He ended his life due to immense work pressures without any help or support available. He was a doctor, caring for others in a stretched system, trying his best. He was unable to go on.

His story is tragic, in that all his life he was revered and respected for his achievements and personality. He was the 'go-to' person if you needed something. He was cultured to devote his life to helping others, but in the end he did so in a state of immense distress and pain. He worked hard for his patients, colleagues, friends and family, but he could not speak openly about the difficulties he faced being a doctor. It was only when he was forcibly signed off work due to stress and anxiety that he opened up about his state of mind, which proved to be fatal and too late. He tried reaching out for help, but there was nothing that could respond to him and keep him safe. He felt alone, isolated and exasperated. His suffering could only be eradicated by the thought of ending his life to escape the torture he was enduring. Immersed in a world where he could not live happily in his environment, nor adapt himself to assimilate into the world around him, the paradox that emerged grew to engulf and ultimately consume him.

I write this today, some years on from his passing, still not believing the way in which he departed this earth. I say to all bereaved by suicide, reflect on your loved one's state of mind and how deep their suffering truly was.

I started a charity called Doctors in Distress to advocate for the protection and maintenance of positive mental health in doctors and all healthcare workers. Our health system appears to have become a psychologically unsafe space in which to work, where adverse mental health and exposure to continued and dangerous levels of stress are an occupational hazard. Society must remember that our caregivers are also human. Disease does not discriminate. Nor should we. Of my (and your) pain, I can only say this. Grief is a substance we all must consume at some time in our lives. It is force-fed to us, and we cannot control our reaction to the poison that enters our mind and body. What makes things easier is knowing that their suffering has ended. The person is gone and is now at peace. Their wish was granted. The acceptance of that is an antidote to the poison of grief. A state of tranquillity is inevitable.

Olly Lavy

There's nothing more important than your family
I wish I held my brother's hand through the agony
Schizophrenia, man, it baffles me.
Mental health is a war zone, and it battles me
My brother had demons in his head, was that consequential?
Or did he just fall victim of his own potential?
Bro had a laugh that was warm and a heart that was pearly
Never been on time, but in the next life, he went early
In this cruel, cruel world, he's the one chosen
But now he rests, and I'm the one frozen
The reason he did that, I guess we'll never know
Can't hold that against him, like Elsa gotta 'Let it go'
See suicide ain't a sprint, it's a relay
Pain gets passed on and you re-play
It's fucked ay…
But death gotta be easy cause life is hard
But the struggle with death is what makes life dark

Scars get deeper than you wouldn't believe
Same time the pain, I don't want it to leave
It's all that I am and I can't get a rest
Same time, I don't wanna get it off my chest
Message after message on my phone
Meantime I've never felt more alone
Friends lookin' out for me, but nobody sees me.
We went through school at a similar age,
But when we speak now I'm on a different page.
Nothing feels the same in conversations,
I watch myself give impersonations,
You start off numb then your bubble gets burst,
I've got envy for those that haven't been cursed.
Is he really hurting or on the fence,
If she's not in pain, then I'm taking offence.
Today it sounds ludicrous,
But I used to be humorous,
Facetious kid, I would take the piss
I feel anger now, and I'm new to this.
Depression's come before,
But I've never been this raw
Ten emotions in an hour, my life's a see-saw
Man, I think I'm going mad again,
It's like I'm happy for a second then I'm sad again.
My eyes burn from the crying and my brain hurts from panicking
My mind's on the dark side, friends call me Anakin
If I look around, I've got no reason to feel bitter
But the feeling that I'm weak, just makes me feel shitter
Swamped everyday like I'm six feet deep
I'm so tired, I'm beyond sleep
Small talk, how are you, that's an awkward question
The feeling of grieving's complex to mention
I feel happy, sad and angry at any one time
The easier response is to just say, I'm fine.

James Mitchell

Leah, my wife of 14 years and mum to our two beautiful boys, Ollie and Harvey, took her own life on 1 May 2020. She was 45 years old. The most tragic and desperately sad day, but not completely unexpected.

Leah had decided from a very early age that every day should be challenged. Sitting still was not an option. There was a whole world out there waiting to be discovered. New people to meet, new tastes to savour. Every day needed to be filled with excitement, adventure and drama. Never really settling for life's somewhat tedious routine. And everyone she met couldn't help but be touched by this magnetic energy.

But lying beneath this fun-loving exterior was a deeply troubled soul. Her childhood had been very traumatic. Daughter to an alcoholic. She would recall drunken fights between her father and older brothers, with her mother seemingly offering little support. Clearly, deep emotional damage had been done – and trust in anyone or anything could never last. But there was something strangely attractive about these fragile insecurities. We had met in 2003 and, quite apart from being drawn to this beautiful and fun-loving, spontaneous girl, I had this overwhelming desire to try to heal. To provide unconditional warmth, love and security. And despite regular explosive outbursts towards me, I wanted to stay the distance – and we married in 2006.

Bringing our first son into the world brought with it an unexpected tragedy. Being infected with a virus during birth caused him severe brain damage, ultimately diagnosed as tetraplegic cerebral palsy. Devastating. Our second son was born two years later – thankfully healthily without any such complications. But this was the start of Leah's slow downward spiral. A wonderful focus and commitment to the boys' upbringing continued to be interspersed with long, dark periods of deep lows, depression and heavy drinking. This became the pattern. Sobriety followed by rehab. Year after year. Including one attempt to end it all. I did my best to shield the boys, but in trying to protect us all I started to normalize this erratic, dysfunctional behaviour. It wasn't until early 2018, many years later, that I had the courage to face reality and to start the emotional detachment.

Slowly realizing that I was no longer going to be there to pick up the pieces, and with both of us recognizing that we needed to separate, Leah moved away from the family home. I continued to support her the best I could, but she was quick to get in with the wrong crowd and soon lost her focus on the boys. Strangely, this new-found resilience and emotional detachment enabled me to secure a significant work promotion. Hugely liberating and yet utterly exhausting, in equal measure.

Those last months of 2019 and early 2020 thankfully brought some peace to Leah's life. She seemed to be working hard on her sobriety and we were able to enjoy Christmas Day together. Mother's Day in March 2020 was the last day we saw her, as lockdown was announced the next day. Not being able to see her boys tore at her deeply. All her demons seemingly returned to haunt her. Five weeks later she drew her last breath.

The first month was a blur of emotions. Huge sadness followed by anger. How dare she. And yet after the funeral, there was a strange sense of relief. For her and for us. Those early months were obviously not easy. But the boys have been incredibly mature. Unbelievably so. Harvey, then only 10, said to me, 'I know I should feel much sadder than I do, but Mum's been living away for over a year now, and I just don't see her much.' Ollie, then 12, was equally matter-of-fact, but this was because of his limited cognition. The school had helped prepare a beautiful 'social story', using easy words and pictures to explain that his mummy had been very sick and had now died. He could remember her by thinking of her favourite colours or singing her favourite songs. He still has this story in his school bag – to look at whenever he needs. We celebrate her life on Mothers' Day and the anniversary of her passing.

How am I? Well, I've been able to take a complete step back from my career so I can fully support my boys. They give me such strength. I still sometimes wake up and expect her to text or call. I'm working hard to get proper balance back in my life. But the skies are clearer and the road ahead, I hope, less traumatic. And sharing my story is bringing yet further closure.

Catherine Morgan

It's very hard to tell people that someone you love took their own life, which is why, sometimes, when I have to explain how I came to be widowed in my early forties, I say my husband died in the pandemic – which is true. My husband Owain Morgan worked as a lawyer for the Welsh Government and in early 2020 he had just been promoted to a managerial role. Unfortunately, just as he was beginning to find his feet, Covid hit, and very soon an alarming series of demands began to land on his desk (now our dining-room table) as he became responsible for drafting new legislation to deal with the pandemic. Not only the scope of the new laws but the speed with which they were introduced was completely unprecedented, and his workload in those early weeks of the first lockdown quickly became impossible. To make things worse, he was someone for whom lockdown itself was immensely difficult to cope with; he would ordinarily have dealt with the stress by heading off on a long walk in the mountains or by the sea; but this was now out of the question.

Soon he suffered a breakdown that left him unable to work at all for extended periods. There ensued several nightmarish months as he struggled with the severe anxiety and depression that followed. It was horrible for him and for me and the children too, and we felt isolated and powerless at a time when medical appointments were hard to come by and we couldn't call on the support of family and friends. During these months there were a few terrifying crises, but other periods when he seemed much better. I always assumed we would make it through our own personal ordeal just as I knew the pandemic couldn't go on forever. By the spring of 2021 I was, like many other people, beginning to feel optimistic again. That Easter we even managed a week's holiday to a different part of Wales. During that week away, Owain seemed more like his old self than he had for a long time, and by the time we arrived back home I was daring to hope that we were through the worst. He had a meeting with his boss scheduled for the following Thursday to discuss returning to work, and when he mentioned that he didn't know how he was going to get through the next few days, I suggested some ideas for things we could do to fill the time. I didn't realize that when someone who has previously felt suicidal begins to seem better that can be a danger sign, and I completely failed to understand the import of his words. The next morning he went out for a walk and smiled and waved at me as he left. That was the last time I saw him alive.

There were many things I found unbearably difficult in the days following Owain's death: first, of course, having to tell our children, and then his parents; then seeing him for the final time at the undertakers on the day that, as it happened, was also our 18th wedding anniversary; having to plan his funeral around the restrictions that meant many of our friends couldn't attend, and then seeing the news reports headlined 'Government lawyer who wrote Covid laws found dead', as if he was somehow to blame. I was told many times not to blame myself, but while I don't feel responsible for the decision he made, I will never be free from the guilt of not being able to save him. There is also the guilt of remembering the times I was angry or impatient with him during those final months when he behaved in ways that were totally irrational or irresponsible; perhaps it was easier to be angry than to accept how unwell he must have been to act so completely out of character. I still find the grief of widowhood very hard to bear: it means trying to deal with heartbreaking loss without the love and support of the one person who could have made it easier. Losing your life partner at a relatively young age also means mourning the loss of the future you had planned together, but because of how he died I began to question our past together too. For nearly 25 years I had believed him to be happy, but I began to wonder whether I had been wrong, and whether I had somehow missed signs of a vulnerability to depression that I had never suspected. What I find hardest of all to accept is that he will never see our children grow up – they are now teenagers and have already changed so much since he died. He would be so proud of them and I'm afraid they will never understand quite how much he loved them.

I wish that I could say something consoling or reassuring about how the journey gets easier. So far this has not been my experience – I feel every day that passes to be another day that my husband should be here to experience with me, but isn't, because I could not help him to find an alternative way out of his despair. I've heard suicide described as 'a permanent solution to a temporary problem' – words that are trite and banal, but sum up for me the tragic waste of a life lost this way. Not long after I was widowed, an older colleague told me how as a young woman she had lost her father to suicide – something she had never told her own children, because it is so hard to admit that someone you love took their own life. She also told me that I would become a stronger person as a result of what I was going through, and reluctantly I admit she was right. In the past few years I have somehow survived pain that I would never have imagined I could endure, and also achieved things I would never have attempted before. I feel I am carrying a very heavy burden and I don't believe it will ever get lighter; all I can say to anyone who feels the same is that as time goes on you adapt and grow stronger, and find that you become more accustomed to the weight.

Josh Smith

You can only stand there in disbelief when someone is taken from you so suddenly. How could you have known that would be the last time you'd see them? My friend Darragh had plans, and no doubt would have been successful in any field he ended up in, as he was an incredibly intelligent man. I'd known Darragh since we were 13. We met in school in our hometown of Newbury and became friends through endlessly quoting our favourite TV shows, then found out we lived just down the road from each other.

The name Darragh comes from the Gaelic word for 'oak tree'. He loved his Irish roots and this would show in everything from his favourite band, Fontaines D.C., to his favourite Irish novelist, James Joyce. Darragh was an avid reader. For the last few years of his life he was studying Politics and International Relations at the London School of Economics and had just completed his degree with first-class honours. Unfortunately, not long after that, Darragh took his life at the age of 26.

I sometimes imagine his smiling face and brilliant laugh sitting next to me when I meet up with our friends, but am reminded so quickly that there is an empty chair at the table and that I will never see my mate again. In the days after Darragh had passed, I couldn't stop thinking to myself, 'Why has this happened? Could I have prevented it? What if I knocked on his door and took him for a coffee? Was I really there for him?' I thought we would have more time – more time to help him. But really there was no time.

These questions will play on my mind forever, but deep down I know that any one of his friends and family would've dropped everything to help him. I believe he knew that. Even if it was just for a moment of laughter to take his mind off things. His family and friends will always remember that beautiful light that once shone from Darragh, as he's left that in our hearts forever.

Here's a song I wrote for Darragh shortly after he passed. I call this song 'Alternate Reality'.

> The coffee's on, a phone goes off, the message hits the room
> With your name, but not from you
>
> A neon light hurts my eyes
> I stare out of the window

Let the tears roll down my cheek
As I just knew

My mother asks if I'm OK
I cry, I lost my friend today

Is there an alternate reality? Where you're still here with me
We could talk about your problems
And get the help you need
Is there a way to wake up from this life as if it were a dream?
This world isn't real to me

Another day, another hour, another passing stranger makes
    me think of you
The way you walked
I see you stood there smiling like
a young oak tree, with roots so deep and leaves that caught
more sunlight than the rest

Why are the best
Always the first ones to fall?
Sometimes the storm is far too strong

Is there an alternate reality where you're still here with me?
We could talk about your problems
And get the help you need
Is there a way to wake up from this life as if it were a dream?
This world isn't real to me

An alternate reality where you're still here with me
We could talk about your problems
And get the help you need
And find a way to wake up from this life as
If it were a dream

This world isn't real to me.

Larissa

Before my family's encounter with suicide I was living a relatively normal life. Whatever normal means. However, little did most people know, including me, that growing deep and painfully inside my mother were the building blocks of depression. I was 17 and can only say what things were like from my own perspective, as no one truly knows what is going on in another's mind. During the years prior, I knew something was different with my mother. A once confident and self-assured person, she now appeared to have lost part of herself. She had mentioned night sweats and I only concluded that, in her late 50s, she was going through menopause.

Tuesday, 11 May 2010. It was a standard afternoon at school, where I was doing athletics on the outdoor track. After the session had finished, I started to walk back towards the school buildings when I noticed my father standing at the side of the field. Instantly, seeing him where he shouldn't be made my heart plummet and a feeling of dread engulfed me. 'Your mother has tried to take her life.'

Over the past 10 years, all we have been able to do is attempt to piece together the reasons my mother took her own life. Needless to say, no one truly knows the reasons apart from her. It is only since her death that I have realized she had depression and I am not sure when this began; whether it was always there but silently hidden, and managed where possible, or if it developed later in life.

The combination of the private nature of my family, the pure, inexplicable grief of losing a parent that way, and the stigma surrounding suicide, resulted in our family deciding we would not make the cause of her death public. Initially, this did make the situation slightly more bearable. However, I strongly believe that in the long term it has made the grieving process even harder, particularly when I consider I might have added to the stigma of suicide. In contrast to the private nature of my parents' personalities, they had brought me up to be open and honest and to wear my heart on my sleeve. Suddenly, in addition to the tumult of emotions of losing my mum through suicide, feeling like I had a hole in my heart, I felt extremely conflicted in not speaking the truth. I could understand why this decision was made and I am sure that is what my mother would have wanted; however, in my mind it felt as though through not being open, I was in some way validating the manner of her death.

As the initial years passed, the truth felt like a huge dark mass building up inside me. That being said, as and when I have felt ready, I have had the courage to confide the truth to a few people close to me and have always found them to be kind, reassuring and sympathetic.

Over the years I have also attempted to understand more about mental health problems and suicide and have tried to use my family's traumatic experience to educate and support others. I have volunteered for Mind charity and through them taken an ASIST (Applied Suicide Intervention Skills Training) course. Throughout my career, which has predominantly been in construction, an industry known for a high level of mental health difficulties and suicide, I have been heavily involved with the promotion of well-being and positive mental health with the aim of encouraging people to speak up and take note of any warning signs of poor mental health and suicide in colleagues, friends and family.

2020 marked a decade since my mother passed away. All I want to do is make her proud, commemorate her memory and try to reach out to mental health sufferers and those affected by suicide. In that year I launched a fundraising campaign, where each month I completed events for three charities that relate to her: Mind, Great Ormond Street Hospital and Cancer Research UK.

Everyone associated with the Time Together service is linked by the painful tragedy of suicide. We have all probably spent many days of our lives trying to understand it. The message I want to deliver is that grief is an individual and highly personal experience and however you grieve is unique to you and your family. Whether you want to talk about it or not is up to you. Whether you want to create charities in memory of a loved one, support existing charities or just remember the person with close family, or in your own mind, that is OK. However you grieve, however you are able to move forward with your life, and perhaps it is keeping yourself constantly busy and occupied like I have, just know this: you are not alone. You have a community right here.

5

Losing the Will to Live

CONTRIBUTORS

Name withheld

I have always thought I could become anything I wanted in life; indeed, in many ways I have achieved everything I wished for. I am a neuroscience researcher, an author, a poet. I have a loving husband and a supportive family. Why would anyone willingly throw them all away? Yet, I tried on several occasions to end my existence – which seemed, to many others, so full of promise and potential.

There was no sadness, no misery, no pain or despair. No tears, no moods or grudges. It was already a state of pure nothingness in my mind and the only thing left for me to do was to reflect such nothingness with my physical absence. An eternal absence, where there would be no self, no volition or will. Then there came the ambivalence and the confusion. Something – someone – was forcing me to do it. I do not believe that anyone is in full control of themselves when they end their own life; I do not believe anyone's sense of reality is intact when they take that final step.

Sadly, this is the reality of suicide. The only reality that engulfed my entire being, the only reality where I could finally be at peace with my own mind, seemed anything *but* my own. So please don't say that I was selfish; there was no self of mine left. Please don't say I was a coward; it required immense strength to override the life instinct. I could be a thought in someone else's head whose termination would have no real-life consequences. I could be a dream within a dream. And all I wanted was to wake up.

If possible, please remember that even in a world of thoughts, you will still need to be alive in order to think; if possible, please remember that even in a state of pure nothingness, you can still hold on to the reality where your true self resides. And that, perhaps, is one of the reasons I am here today.

Counterbalance

I see the brilliance in a passionate life,
I see my future ahead of me
I must continue living
To reach the final destination

I hear the voices of logic and reason
I hear the noises of my cells withering,
I must die again and again
To prove that life is infinite
An incomplete paradox
I saw the trails of a crimson tide
I saw the amorphous clouds in the sky
Should I keep flying, or should I descend?

I heard the thunders underneath my skin I
heard the painful songs of my brain
Can I sign a full stop, or can I win the fight?

A subconscious dichotomy

I will see the nightmares of a child
I will see the wings of time and space
Maybe they are not my own thoughts
Maybe I am just one step away

I will hear the melody of the ending
I will hear the isolated laughter from my psyche
Only if I was closer to the edge
Only if I wasn't denied reality
A perfect counterbalance.

James Withey

My name is James Withey. I've lost friends to suicide and I almost lost myself. I went from delivering suicide prevention training to being on 5-minute suicide watch in a psychiatric hospital. In 2010 I moved from Scotland to Brighton with my partner, a stressful move in itself; but then things started to unravel. I couldn't find work, we couldn't get a mortgage again, my partner was made redundant and had to take a job in

Ireland, only coming back every other weekend. When I did find work, it was teaching part-time in health and social care at a further education college (my background is in addiction and training).

A few months after starting the job, I was teaching another class and had to discipline a female student who was breaking college rules. A few days later I was told she had accused me of sexual misconduct. I was shattered. My sleep started to be affected, I couldn't concentrate, found it hard to cope. I kept crying, had panic attacks and felt displaced. When a new full-time job turned out to be a huge mistake, I had constant thoughts of suicide. I made plans to kill myself the following week and I broke.

Suicidal thoughts happen when pain exceeds resources. All I could feel was pain and I needed a way for it to stop: nothing else mattered. I started walking in front of cars, getting dangerously close to passing trains and eventually taking an overdose of sleeping pills. I went to A&E where the first doctor I saw couldn't look me in the eyes when I told her I wanted to kill myself. After a six-hour wait, the mental health nurse I saw told me I was too sensitive and I was sent home. The following day I went to my GP, who sighed as if I was wasting his time. When I said I was still suicidal he called the crisis team and told me to sit in the corridor to wait for them.

One of the training courses I used to deliver was called ASIST. It helps people intervene when someone is at risk of killing themselves. This is how I heard about Maytree. In my darkest hour I called them and made plans to stay. I needed a place where I could talk about my suicidal thoughts, where I didn't feel ashamed of my thoughts and had space to look at what had happened to me and maybe how I could keep living. Maytree is truly a sanctuary; I was cared for, meals prepared, a comfortable bed and support on tap; but I also had my independence. I could cycle around London, see family and had my medication with me. This contrasts with my time in a psychiatric hospital after a suicide attempt, which felt like a necessary prison.

One night I felt very suicidal, I wanted to leave, I wanted to run in front of a car; a Maytree volunteer sat with me. He didn't barricade me in, he didn't phone the police. He just sat with me, he told me he wanted me to stay, he listened, he was beside me. I felt that I could never recover from depression or my experiences, but during a one-to-one session with a worker she told me she thought I had been crushed, but not obliterated; and some light started to seep through. These two events stand out to me during my time as catalysts for change, but so did the empathy and care of every volunteer and staff member; the offer of a drink, a smile, giving me eye contact and seeing me as James, as a fellow human who was hurt but still here and valid. They saw me as having worth when I despised myself.

My life after Maytree has been up and down but it gave me crucial hope. It spoke to the life part of me as well as the part whose soul had been crushed. It gave me a foundation for recovery. I now work part-time in a library. I write, I cycle, I try to remember who I am, not the depression that I suffer from. I think about those who didn't make it.

We are all few steps away from suicidal thoughts and actions. We need more places like Maytree, spaces where people can go and talk about their trauma. We need to stop the shame of suicidal thoughts and suicide itself. We need to work together, support one another and remember those who have left us. We need to come together, because suicide separates us from those that we love. We need to realize that stressful life events and mental health issues are life-threatening illnesses. We need to make sure that when the stick breaks there are people and places to help us start to mend it.

These words are for Neil, who really tried to make it and couldn't.

Jonny Benjamin MBE

I was about 16 years old when I first began to contemplate suicide. At the age of ten I started hearing a voice in my head – I believed it was the voice of an angel, and I liked the voice being there. It was something of a companion. When I turned 16 though, the voice changed from an angel to a devil and began to torment me. It challenged me to do certain things, or else I would be punished. Suddenly, living inside my head became unbearable. Added to this were my increasingly low moods. They would come without warning and completely take over me. Sometimes I would feel overcome with so much emotion that I had no choice but to cry. Often there would be no reason, no trigger for it. And always I suffered secretly, in silence.

Simply put, I was embarrassed and ashamed. 'You shouldn't be feeling like this,' I kept telling myself. As a result, everything was kept firmly locked inside.

It's amazing how much pain and suffering we can endure, and more than that, how much of it we can mask. Not only was I hiding my mental turmoil, but I had begun to struggle with my sexuality too.

Coming from a Jewish community where I was told that to be gay was a sin, I started to consider a way of escaping this existence I was living. The first time I actually considered suicide, I was sitting in the back of my parents' car, aged 16, driving to a family function. We passed by a graveyard. 'I want to be in there,' I said to myself. There was a sense of peace I saw in that graveyard that seemed so far removed from me as I sat in the car, full of hatred and anger and despair for myself.

But the worst was still to come. During the next four years I passed my GCSEs, A levels, driving test and got a place at a prestigious drama school. Acting – particularly that transformation into other characters – proved a chance for me to escape from myself. Without it, I think I would have broken down much earlier. But all the achievements my family and friends saw on the outside was a total contrast to what was happening to me internally. I turned to self-harm and alcohol while trying various antidepressants. I spiralled gradually out of control. By the first term of my third year, I could no longer contain the burden of everything I was holding onto and I broke down, going onto a dual carriageway near my student house and walking down the central reservation of it. I was psychotic, out of control and suicidal. I was eventually taken to A&E, and sometime after that admitted to a psychiatric hospital, where I was diagnosed with schizoaffective disorder – a combination of schizophrenia and bipolar.

I spent a month in the hospital before I decided to run away and end my life. There were lots of factors in my decision to do this – my sexuality, stigma, shame and embarrassment (yet again); but the prevailing factor was my belief that I would never ever recover. These are the words of a poem I wrote to describe how this felt.

> I wish that I could tell you, I'm longing to explain,
> Because the day-to-day would be easier,
> If I could share a little of this pain.
> It's not the words I'm looking for,
> I have them all right here.
> It's the courage I need to say them,
> That is buried deep within my fear.
> The fear of what you'll think,
> The fear of what might change,
> Or, maybe, it's the fear in me,
> That I'll never find what I've lost again.

And that was exactly it – I convinced myself I was broken, unrepairable and past the point of no return. So on 14 January 2008, just before my 21st birthday, I ran away from the hospital and came to a bridge near here to jump from the edge of it. But while on the edge, I met a young man who tried to talk me down. Through his empathy, kindness, patience and compassion, and through his constant repetition of the simple statement, 'Mate, I really believe you'll get better,' he changed my mind about what I was about to do. Someone, a stranger, believed so strongly in me at a point when I had absolutely no faith left in myself.

That was the moment I found hope and the point my recovery started. The last eight years have been tough at times. I've relapsed, been hospitalized and become suicidal again. But I've also been able to achieve things along the way. I led a successful campaign to find the stranger on the bridge. It went viral and reunited me with the Good Samaritan, Neil Laybourn. Recently I launched a new mental health charity, Beyond, which is going down really well. I now go into places like hospitals, prisons and businesses to share my experiences and encourage others to talk. I want to do all I can to break the shame and silence around mental health, and especially suicide.

On the way up to the bridge that day, I prayed desperately for my family. I prayed the whole way there. I said, 'God, I don't want them to feel guilty or responsible in any way.' I later added a final verse to the above poem.

> What if it has gone, never to come back?
> Not all things return once apart.
> Well then, we'll just create a new beginning.
> There's no limit to the infinite times we can restart.

Rohan Kallicharan

Norman Cousins, an American political activist and journalist, was given a mere few months to live back in 1964; he finally left this life in 1990, having written a collection of books on illness and healing. His story is one of survival, of healing, and yet I believe so pertinent when we speak of loss and, especially, suicide. He says, 'Death is not the greatest loss in life. The greatest loss is what dies inside us while we live.' This evoked in me a great deal of reflection and self-examination, a look back to a time when I didn't want to be here, when every tomorrow was one too far.

I have lived with Bipolar Disorder Type 1 since my late teens; it was undiagnosed for close to 15 years – a period during which I lived on a rollercoaster, on which I either loved or absolutely despised myself. At the height of the illness, I hadn't the mental capacity to make rational decisions; I wasn't overly concerned by stigma, I was just scared to speak out of self-hatred – why would anyone listen to anything I had to say? Every external sign looked like anti-social, erratic, irresponsible behaviour; without the awareness of mental illness we have now, that is all I saw and others saw. With each increasingly volatile moment, I died a little. I never considered that I was ill; I just thought it was me, that I was a social leper, an untouchable on a one-way road to isolation and self-destruction.

My first suicide attempt was a call for help, which never came. Life continued and, left untreated, the illness continued to destroy me, cutting into every vein, a destructive decaying influence on what was a shell, a human body on the outside, annihilated and obliterated within. As Cousins says, the loss is what dies in us while we live, and bipolar had stripped me of my life, self-respect and dignity. The towel had been thrown in and God would forgive me – he alone knew how broken I was at the pain being caused to those I loved. By the time of the third and final attempt on my life in January 2006, I meant it.

Even now, I can only attribute it to God's grace that the person who woke up the next morning actually wanted to live. I didn't know how to, but for the first time in 15 years was clinging on to a forlorn hope. In recovery and diagnosis, there was a real sense of loss. I was a small child, learning how to live and function again, and while my life with illness had been destructive, it was all I had known in my adult life; I was leaving the comfort and familiarity of illness and life as I knew it behind. It was a frightening but positive loss.

Like with any child, the journey took time. I had to learn to live with being well, those around me had to learn to trust this child and let him live and flourish. It was close to five years before I realized God had given me a purpose and the opportunity to change lives. I had walked through the valley of the shadow of death but now feared no evil. Perhaps in my recovery the one person I had never forgiven was myself – for the pain I'd caused others. I found myself drawn to the words of the prophet Isaiah: 'Do not fear, for I have redeemed you; I have summoned you by name; you are mine.' And yes, I felt deeply guilty, which was driven by the fact that I'd lived, when so many others hadn't. It is now replaced by a purpose to reach out and change the lives of others.

Cousins famously says, 'If something comes to life in others because of you, then you have made an approach to immortality.' I have no desire for immortality: eternal life is mine in Christ alone. However, every day is underpinned by bringing something to life in others. I hope you find the comfort of knowing your loved ones perhaps had lost everything inside them while they lived and that is why they felt they had nothing left. And when that feeling of darkness, loss and emptiness permeates within, all the love and brightness you radiate might be futile.

I know that together we can all continue working to create a world where we bring that light and hope to them before it is too late. Cousins says, 'The capacity for hope is the most significant fact of life. It provides human beings with a sense of destination and the energy to get started.' We must provide that hope to current and future generations.

Jake Mills

I am just a normal lad who made mistakes, lived a lie, and eventually, after battling with depression, attempted to take my own life in 2013. I didn't ever think I would be someone who suffered from depression. I certainly didn't ever imagine I would be someone who would attempt suicide. But depression got me out of nowhere. It crept up and pulled me apart bit by bit.

There were many reasons for my struggle, some rational, some irrational, and some completely out of my control. The best way to describe how I felt is as if I lived inside a bubble. I may have appeared as living in the outside world, but I was cut off from it all. I became numb to everything: thoughts, feelings, emotions. I knew I should feel a certain way: my head would tell me but my heart couldn't feel it. Every day I felt as if I was treading water, battling to stay afloat. Some days I would stay above, some days I would go under. But every day seemed like an effort. I was drowning. I was helpless. I couldn't escape and no matter how they tried, no one could help me. I felt devastatingly alone, despite support around me. I was lost, worthless, without a purpose. A burden to everyone around me.

I began to live a life inside my own head. I became a different person. I didn't want to mix with people, I didn't want to go out. Things I enjoyed before I had no time for. My parents and girlfriend knew that something was wrong, but the more they asked me how I was or offered to help, the more it pushed me away. I felt as though I was a burden to them. I didn't think I could be helped, so I didn't want them to waste their time trying.

I didn't think I could be helped. Nothing sums up my journey and that of many others more than that one sentence. I didn't know. I didn't know I was depressed. I didn't *really* know what depression was. I didn't know there was help. I didn't know there was a way through. But then, why would I? Why would I know what depression was? How would I be aware of the signs and symptoms, the feelings I could feel? How would I know the process of recovery if nobody had ever taught me? How would I know that what I was feeling was incredibly common if I had never been prepared? Quite simply, I couldn't and I didn't. It has taken a near-fatal suicide attempt for me to understand how wrong I was. It has taken me speaking publicly about my battles to realize I wasn't alone. That is just not good enough.

I genuinely believed that by killing myself, I would be doing the best for me and for my family. I felt that, yes, they would be sad, but their lives would improve without having me there to worry about. It was only after I was found and I had to face my mum, to see my dad's face, that I realized just how wrong I was. I started to speak publicly about my battles, and very quickly I had my eyes opened to the amount of needless suffering that goes on around us all every single day. People battling away in secret, millions of people thinking the exact same things at the exact same time, all feeling like they are the only one. People having no idea how to deal with their issues, feeling as though there is nowhere to turn. So quickly, people started to turn to me, purely because I had shared my own experiences. They started to see hope. Hope in somebody coming out the other side. But more importantly, hope in somebody who would understand.

I am incredibly privileged to still be here. I know and appreciate that every single day. But just talking about my experiences is not good enough. It comes with a responsibility and with that responsibility I have found myself with a chance to help make a difference. I would say one of the biggest differences between poor physical health and poor mental health, is that if it is physical, we know, understand and trust the process to get well again. If it is mental, we don't know it, we don't understand it and we certainly don't trust it.

According to the latest stats, nearly three-quarters of those who died by suicide were not known to mental health services or had not been in touch with services for more than a year. That is outrageous. There is clearly a fundamental issue with either how the services work or how we publicize who and what they are. We cannot sit by and allow it to continue to happen. We cannot allow politics or rivalry or money fly in the face of helping those who need it the most. That is why I founded a national charity, Chasing the Stigma, and built and launched the Hub of Hope, which is a first-of-its-kind mental health database of services and support that can be found at the click of a button. We have to make the support as easy as possible to find. We have to give people options, and we have to be as loud and obnoxious about it as we need to be. Because I would say, having the options and never using them is just as important as if you do.

We will work towards a world where speaking out about the issues you have faced is no longer considered to be a brave act. It should be a normal thing that we all do. There is no quick solution, but if we are prepared to make a change then a change will come.

Gill Hayes

Many people remember 2012: the Queen's Diamond Jubilee, the London Olympics. I remember 2012 for a different reason: for me, it was the year things started to unravel. The previous year, I had moved to Devon with my family for a better quality of life: we planned to 'live the dream'. Things had started well. The children had settled well into their new schools, and we had met some lovely people. There was a series of setbacks in our new life, but nothing I thought I couldn't handle.

However, a year into our time in Devon, I realized that things weren't quite right. I'd started waking really early. Things that I'd previously enjoyed, I didn't want to do. I was becoming withdrawn; social occasions were a real effort. My concentration levels were flagging, my thinking was becoming muddled, making simple decisions became really difficult. What was going on? I googled my symptoms. The diagnosis came back: depression. Depression! Me! How embarrassing! What did I have to be depressed about? Pull yourself together!

After a few months it became obvious that I wasn't doing a terribly good job at pulling myself together. Too ashamed to speak to my GP, I contacted the local Depression and Anxiety Service. They recommended a course of Cognitive Behavioural Therapy and, as time progressed, my depression lifted. I started to laugh again, to enjoy things again, I could concentrate and engage with people. It was such an enormous relief. With hindsight, this would have been a good time to reflect, to work out what had contributed to my depression and make some adjustments to my life. But I didn't. So relieved to be out of the hellhole that is depression, I decided to make up for lost time. It was time to come back and suck the juice out of life. I was never going back to that dark place.

A few months later however, the depression returned. This time the descent was much more rapid, and it hit me much, much harder. I couldn't do the simplest of things: a trip to the supermarket was overwhelming, I stopped opening my post, my emails. I had no appetite. I tried to keep up appearances, but it was hard work. So I started to avoid people. I just seemed to shut down.

My concerned husband made me see a doctor. I was given a questionnaire to gauge the severity of my depression. My answers confirmed that it was indeed severe, but I lied on the last two questions – the ones about suicide. How could I confess to feeling suicidal? What if they take away my children? The doctor prescribed antidepressants and said they might make me feel worse before I felt better. Worse?! Worse than this? I wasn't taking them. And taking them would be proof of my failure to sort this out myself.

I noticed the way I was behaving was starting to impact on my children. Unable to concentrate or function properly, I couldn't give them the usual levels of attention and support. My mind corroded by depression, I reached the point where I thought that this thing that was destroying me would take my family down too. I would not let that happen. Each morning I would wake at 1am. I would lie there for hours telling myself how pathetic I was, what a coward I was for still being here, a burden to my family. I would be disgusted with myself by sunrise for still existing. This had to stop.

In mid-March 2013, I went to bed and, as usual, woke at 1am. No backing out this time, you have to do this. Don't stop, don't think, don't kiss them goodbye ... I got out of bed, left my sleeping family, drove to a nearby bridge and jumped. I don't remember the fall or the impact. I remember being found, I remember a neck brace being fitted and being put into the ambulance. As I was being taken to hospital, two policemen would knock at my front door and break the news to my husband. From there the news would spread, causing shock and disbelief. 'How could you do this to your children?' 'Why?' 'Maybe I didn't really know you after all.' Natural thoughts for loved ones in the wake of such an event. How could I expect anyone to understand that I had done this from a place of love – wanting them to be free from the burden I had become? Maybe that's not possible to understand unless you have been there yourself. Viewing the situation through the prism of a healthy mind, not understanding the caustic nature of severe depression, not understanding how it warps your thinking, suicide does indeed seem unfathomable.

While in hospital, physically broken, mentally and emotionally at rock bottom, I received a gift from a 10-year-old boy, George, a school friend of my son. It was a hand-knitted bookmark with a single word stitched onto it – 'Hope'. George had summed up in one word what I so badly needed at that time. Hope is in short supply when you are depressed. Severe depression is a place of complete, total and utter despair. I needed to understand that I'd been extremely ill and I needed hope that I could and would recover. Hope in our darkest times is not always easy to find. That vital ingredient for healing, for moving forward, can so easily elude us. I was lucky to find hope. Wherever you are on your journey, through love, understanding and coming together, I hope you can find it too.

Conor Stainton-Polland

I have to resist running into the vestry behind me, throwing on some robes and beginning, 'The Lord be with You.' Because, yes, I'm a clergyman – 21 years a Catholic priest. A few years ago, I was promoted by my archbishop to Dean of North Liverpool. The name of one of my Liverpool districts allows me to proudly say – I am the Dean of Kensington! OK, my Kensington is a little bit different and my area also encompasses Knotty Ash where Ken Dodd's Diddy Men come from – yes, it's a real place, and I do love 'happiness' – not just the song, but the emotion.

I introduce myself like that to highlight that it can be anyone: 'it' being mental health issues. I'm like a miserable National Lottery advert, 'It could be you!' My love for happiness sometimes gets out of control, and my acquaintance with its darker sibling, sorrow and depression, can overtake me as well. Around the same time I was made dean, I was diagnosed as bipolar and, as I say, there are only two ways to react to a diagnosis of bipolar: 'Yay!' and 'Oh.'

I was and am glad of the diagnosis. It explains why sometimes I just can't stop working and getting things done – those days when emptying my office bin ends hours later with an entirely spotless house from top to bottom. But better yet it explains my darknesses, those horrible, lonely, crushing times of depression when there is nothing of me but a black hole sucking in and obliterating any light.

I think if you can describe depression then it's not depression you're suffering from. I've had three first cousins die by suicide and I've been with many families who have lost a loved one to suicide and I've been there for that moment of silence and bleakness descending that surrenders to no definition. If it did, it would maybe be easier to overcome. It's the unspoken paradox of suicide that those left in its miasmic wake end up themselves exploring, entering into, that very darkness they're trying to understand – the darkness that's taken their loved one.

You get it, don't you? That darkness, where the soul hurts, the agony that is isolating even when hand-in-hand with a loved one. Is it any wonder people can fall away from each other in this silence and pain? Any wonder there's separation and breakdown? It seems so isolating, but I want us to dare to see it as another paradox: it's putting us in actual touch with our lost loved ones, in touch with their moment of literal, literal, madness.

I can say madness. As a manic depressive I can claim any of those words that I like and I claim it for this: that madness we feel in that emptiness communicates to us the dreadful numbness our loved ones felt and could not escape or overcome. That shared experience of the madness is then absolution, hard-won in passion and agony. By your own darkness you know, you know, you could have done nothing or said nothing or been nothing to break the impenetrable.

People in recent decades have frowned so much at the phrase 'I understand' that empathy 101 has demanded we never say it. But I suggest we dare to say it – 'I understand.' I understand your pain and we understand their pain.

Almost exactly three years ago I lay on my sofa with the throw covering me from head to toe, immobile. I'd closed off what senses I could, because I feared what I would do if I let myself move; because I knew what I would do if I let myself move. It hurt so much. Every inch of me was darkness. Every cell of mind and heart and body vibrated with hopelessness. Staff were in the house, just the other side of my living room wall. An hour to go till they left. I told myself that if I felt the same as they shouted, 'Goodbye, Father,' then I'd move. I'd make that move. I'd make the move. Trembling, agonized, lost I lay. 'Father?' Oh no, I was about to be called for some essential parochial or pastoral duty. I was going to be called to give the last rites to someone and envy them as they got to escape. 'Father?' I tried to breathe normally enough to answer, 'Yes.'

'Father, the school just rang, could you kick their football back over the fence please?'

Some people's last acts are heroic, mine was to be, well … instead of 'Priest brings many comfort, then dies,' I would be 'Priest kicks ball then dies.'

I moved.

Motion began.

Into the back yard and the drizzle, finding the ball, kicking it over the fence, picking it up when it bounced back at me off the fence, kicking it again: this time it makes it over; turning and looking back to an indoors that was to be an end. A step, another, then I slipped, falling on damp decking, falling – and arms shoot out to protect myself. They stop me, my forehead an inch away from the corner of a lead planter; my arms and instincts saved me an inch from death. The perfect accidental death thwarted by instinct. And I laughed, I laughed at the devil, I laughed at myself. Will and instinct resumed, for life at least, their proper chain of command. My rope broke. My pills ran out. My train was late. My moment, that day, passed.

So I'll dare to say I understand. I understand your darkest moment, don't shut me out. I understand their darkest moment, don't shut me out. With that understanding comes companionship and that breaks the isolation like arms thrown out to break a fall.

Arms thrown out to break a fall.

'I understand,' don't we?

6

Walking Alongside

CONTRIBUTORS

Paddy Bazeley

One way or another, helping distressed and, particularly, suicidal people became my career. I'm not really sure how, except it might have had something to do with being a Brownie when I was 7 or 8 and was an 'Irish Leprechaun helping people when forlorn'.

It's all seemed a matter of luck – an odd word to use, perhaps – but, beginning with thinking of doing a bit of voluntary work, and being encouraged by a friend to apply to the Samaritans, I applied to be a volunteer in 1972 and then went on to work full time in various roles, but essentially seeing people who'd contacted the Samaritans, and exploring with them what help they needed and then helping them find it. I left the Samaritans in 2000 to set up Maytree – a sanctuary for the suicidal. Over the years I'd met so many people for whom suicide had become an option (not a choice) as they struggled to solve a problem, whether a material one such as debt or redundancy, or an emotional one, such as a breakdown of a relationship or a bereavement, or something less easily defined but probably described as 'depression', and as often as not, a combination of more than one of these.

I came to understand that we all have a knowledge of suicide within us, and given a certain set of circumstances, suicide can seem the only way out; and for some it might be. For most, however, the problem – however apparently intractable – can be managed, sorted out. The dilemma of whether to live or die is resolved and life can go on, albeit with a wound, and the knowledge that life can be very fragile.

Sometimes, however, the problem seems insurmountable, and all efforts seem wasted. Negative and pessimistic thoughts take over: 'What is the point when I'm going to die anyway'; 'I don't want to burden anyone'; 'They'll be better off without me'; 'They don't really care'. The list is endless. Typically, such a person becomes more withdrawn, more introverted as they become preoccupied with negative ruminations and move to a deeper level of the life/death dilemma. Yet, amazingly, some manage to maintain a mask of 'There's nothing wrong'; 'Don't fuss'; they may trivialize it: 'I'm just a bit down'; 'I'm not going to do anything stupid'; which, of course, makes their death all the more of a shock. Shocking, perplexing and inexplicable, leaving so many questions that can't be answered. And you are left having to learn to live with not knowing.

I joined the Samaritans to 'save people' – a common mistake in the early days of working in a caring profession. But I know, all these years later, that people can survive a suicidal crisis, and I have been privileged to experience probably several hundred people who *have* negotiated that most fundamental question, 'What is the point of life?' or 'Is it worth it – is it worth going through this unbearable pain?' and have decided, 'Yes.' I wouldn't be writing this if I didn't believe that people can survive, and go on to live fruitful and fulfilled lives.

There have been many beautiful and often funny times at Maytree, but one of the most memorable was our first Christmas. We had two guests, a young female student who'd taken a serious overdose, and an elderly Indian gentleman who'd been pulled out of the Thames. Both had been taken to St Thomas's Hospital and then referred to Maytree. My colleague, Michael, an excellent cook, had made supper, and the four of us sat round the kitchen table talking. The young woman said something about why she had wanted to die, and the elderly Indian gentleman just broke down and said he had lived with the same fear for years, and had thought he was the only one who felt like that – and he'd decided that he couldn't go on any longer. The knowledge that he wasn't mad and that he wasn't alone with these thoughts made the difference to both of them. A memorable Christmas indeed.

One Maytree guest who'd been found unconscious in a quiet corner of a big London park and then had come to Maytree said this (and I quote with permission): 'I came here in a thousand pieces, without hope, in terror, and in total despair, wanting to die. I had made the decision to die. I leave here as a whole person no longer in pieces, with hope and knowing that I can change. I have the will to live.' I hope I've given you a sense of the power of suicide, that no one makes that decision lightly, that sometimes it is the only way; but also that people can survive and that if you have lost someone to suicide, you too can survive.

Ruth Kloocke

I feel a great sense of responsibility. I am honoured to contribute from the perspective of a mental health professional affected by suicide. It is an important task, but also a daunting one. It feels – as so often, when I do my job – like walking a tightrope, where I have to tread carefully and every word matters. I have worked as a psychiatrist for more than 20 years. Much of my work is alive with a sense of optimism. I never cease to be in awe of the power of human connection. I am in awe of the moment when people share who they are and how they feel with – often – total strangers, and something happens: where people can start to make sense of their experiences and stories and start to build a sense of 'being seen' and 'being heard' and 'not alone'. This is where the optimism comes from, and where a sense of possibility and hope arises.

To me this often happens in the non-verbal domain of 'being seen' – it feels to me that the way I look at somebody, the way I make eye contact, the way I take somebody in, the way I connect to their physical presence by 'seeing' makes all the other steps of healing and recovering and rebuilding possible. It is inevitable that this process of 'seeing' is a mutual process of 'being seen'. I can't do this work without allowing myself to be seen – without allowing the person I am trying to connect with to look at me in the very same way. They will know more about me than I imagine. They will 'read' me and will know of me, often in a subtle and non-explicit way, simply by being with me for an hour or so.

This is where the experience of suicide and the mere possibility of a person ending their life come in. They will know if I feel scared. They will know if I am sad. They will know if I respect their freedom to make decisions or if I propose to make decisions on their behalf. There is no hiding in this moment of connecting with somebody. And there is no way I can be sure that I will get it right. There is no way I can do this work without 'not knowing' if I get it right. Most of the time I will *not* know, but will have to trust myself. I have to trust my attentiveness, my sense of integrity, seriousness and honesty, and willingness to question myself.

And if it happens – if somebody takes their life – again, there is the 'not knowing'. There is no way I will know or find out what happened for the person in the moment they made this decision. I will have to live and carry on with this 'not knowing'. I will have to carry on trusting myself, trusting my colleagues and trust the moment of connection, when optimism starts, and 'life' as opposed to 'death' or 'suicide' becomes thinkable. That's the moment I want to talk about. What happens if somebody decides to take their life – or if it happened in a moment of impulse and feeling lost. It feels like a physical blow to hear about somebody having died in this way.

I have asked a family for permission to talk about how I have been affected by their son's death, A. I realize that I think of A with a sense of disbelief that he is no longer here. I 'see' him everywhere. When I see slight red-haired men in their late thirties or early forties, I think of him. As part of the formal process following the unexpected death of a person, I had to read all of A's clinic notes. The task gave me great solace. It felt like honouring, remembering and again taking in who he was as a person. Stopping. Making sense of it all. And making time for sadness. Sadness.

I can't say how much I value that A's family took time to talk to us – the clinicians involved in A's care in the months prior to his death – after he died. I can't say how much I admired their courage to share their sorrow and anger and despair with us. Being invited to A's funeral felt like a gift. Like an opportunity to find closure in the midst of all the sadness and despair. Hearing A's sister speaking with a lot of love about how 'infuriating' A could be made me feel immensely happy. It made me feel that I had actually 'seen' the person they had seen. And made me realize how much he was 'seen' and appreciated in his life and in his death.

Suicide is contagious. Suicide is carried in the fear and lack of connectedness following on from it – the black hole of despair and self-doubt that follow on from it. And only these acts of connection enable us professionals to carry on with the uncertainty of 'not knowing' but 'seeing' and 'connecting'. These acts of connection enable me again to 'see' people in my professional capacity with a sense of optimism and hope while allowing them to 'see' me as the person I am – often immensely sad, but not without hope.

I want persons and families who have lost somebody through suicide to know how important you are to us professionals – how much your *willingness* to talk can help us to carry on and make sense of it all.

Joy Hibbins

In March 2012, a traumatic experience changed my life. I developed symptoms of post-traumatic stress disorder: flashbacks, nightmares and intrusive thoughts. On around the third day, I started to develop an inexplicable fear, which left me unable to sit with my back to a door. I was convinced that something or someone would come in and harm me. Eventually, I perceived that the source of my fear was upstairs. I had started to believe that there were dark forces – malevolent forces – in my home. The traumatic experience had destabilized my mind, triggering a psychotic episode. I had no previous history of psychosis or serious mental illness.

After a period under the mental health crisis team, I was referred for psychological therapy. I was told that the waiting time would be at least eight months. In the end, it was even longer. During that period, my mental health continued to deteriorate, and my untreated symptoms became ever more severe. It felt that there was no escape from the traumatic event. I was constantly reliving it through flashbacks and intrusive thoughts. Death increasingly represented an escape route.

As I descended deeper into suicidal crisis, I could no longer hold my loved ones in my mind. I became detached and disconnected. It was as if everyone and everything that mattered to me was on some distant horizon, outside my field of vision. My suicidal intent was a dark tunnel now. There was nothing else apart from that tunnel – that focused intent to end my life. I could see nothing but the final destination. I attempted suicide, but survived.

My own experience of suicidal crisis gave me a deep understanding of what it is like to be in crisis. And my experiences of being under mental health services led me to understand that some of us need a different kind of care. I had encountered clinical distance from mental health professionals, and that left me detached, disconnected and unreachable. I had also felt powerless and disempowered under services. I wanted to set up a crisis service which was very different; where kindness and care replace clinical distance and where we place clients in control as much as possible.

In 2013 I set up a suicide crisis centre, which is open to anyone who is feeling suicidal. We also run a separate trauma centre, which provides early intervention to try to help prevent a descent into crisis. In the period since that we have been providing services, there has never been a suicide of a client under our care.

It became clear that we would need to provide additional services, too. Daniel, our very first client, had been through an extremely harrowing experience five weeks earlier and was too afraid and too traumatized to leave the home, so we had to go out to him. This showed us that we would need to provide home visits for some clients. We now provide a combination of suicide crisis centre, home visits and emergency phone lines for our clients.

The strong connection we build with clients is so important. I recall the night when another client, Alan, was on his way to a location to end his life, walking across fields in driving rain. I took the call from him on the night emergency line. He could barely speak initially. He hadn't wanted to call, he told us later. It was the connection he had built with us which led him to make that call. It was as if an unbreakable cord kept him attached to us. Now we are approached by people in different parts of the UK, who want to set up similar suicide crisis centres or indeed new initiatives of their own. It is so often their own lived experience which drives them.

A traumatic experience may devastate our lives and we may lose so much. We are never the same, subsequently. We grieve for all that we have lost; our loved ones, the loss of our past life, and perhaps even the loss of our past self. But the inner core that defines us can re-emerge. It is still there, buried deep within us. And the experience of trauma can eventually allow us to find within ourselves qualities and abilities we never knew that we had. The person I was before 2012 could never have set up a suicide crisis centre. After the trauma, I developed a determination, a tenacity and a drive which I had never experienced before. When other people spoke in terms of, 'If you set up a suicide crisis centre,' I never corrected them. But I knew it was a case of 'when' and not 'if'. It simply had to be set up.

I am sometimes asked if my work has a detrimental impact on me. It has the opposite effect. Although it is complex, challenging and demanding work, it is enormously hopeful. We absolutely believe that all our clients can survive. And we see such wonderful qualities in them. We know that they are going to impact positively on other people in the future. When they talk about the future, many of them say that their greatest wish now is to help other people. Their lived experience will be a powerful means to enable them to do that.

7

Finding Solidarity on the Journey after Suicide

DAVID MOSSE

Each year between 2015 and 2022, except for 2021, the year of Covid, I had the honour of giving an opening address for the Time to Talk (Time Together) service, at which around 500 people gathered at St Martin-in-the Fields. Those short talks are put together here. Each service was structured as a journey in three parts: 'Lost', 'the Valley' and 'Found'. First, the experience of *lostness*: the tragic loss of self, loss of worth, of hope, of trust, of human connectedness that precedes suicide; and the terrible loss of those bereaved by suicide. Second, the experience of exhaustion, depletion and isolation that can impede the road to recovery, or lead to unresolved grief. In this imagined high-sided *valley*, guilt, stigma and self-blame are among the obstacles placed before those who suffer a loss of self or the loss of loved ones, making it hard to reach out for help. The final part of the journey through the service is about being *found*, signifying the recovery of self through connection to others, living with loss, remembering with gratitude and allowing our grief to become part of our living, healing and hopefulness.

Another reality (2015)

Today, five years ago, my beloved son Jake was, I now realize, planning his own imminent end. Neither I nor any of his closest of friends, nor his brother who was so dear to him, could have imagined that this loving, talented young man would contemplate his own death. Jake is not with us to explain why he felt there was no other choice available to him (when we can see so many); and even now his suicide has an unreality about it. Those here who have experienced this terrible bereavement will understand what I mean when I say that for me one reality ended that day; and another reality began.

Suicide tore through and ruptured the story of my life and of my family, as it has for so many. For a moment, I imagined that I experienced a shadow of the pain that made Jake himself think of oblivion. We will listen to beautiful music in this service, but there is absolutely nothing beautiful about suicide.

I not only face the deep sadness of the loss of my darling son, but have a second – sometimes overpowering – grief for the manner in which he died: his suicide. Out of the trauma and confusion of suicide comes the repeated question, why? How could this have happened? Why was he not stopped? We may ask whether we truly knew the person who is gone. How could distress so deep as to lead to suicide be invisible? We look back painfully to try to name the 'warning signs' that hindsight offers, we ruminate on the 'if onlys'; suicide leaves us unbearably powerless. But there are no reliable signs of impending suicide; every suicide comes as a shock. If we are not careful, as we strain to explain, suicide can colour the memory of those we loved, robbing us of their past as well as their future.

Like others, I've begun a lifelong search for understanding. I've learned about the distorting mental processes of severe depression, the fragility of male strength, the dangers of perfectionism, of self-worth conditional on achievements, the perils of isolation, entrapment and fear of humiliation. I've learned that humans are moved to self-harm both by passing impulsiveness and by deeper drumbeats of the psyche of which we are hardly aware. I'm no expert, but I've also learned some things that suicide probably is not: it's not a choice as we normally understand choice, but comes out of a state of mind simply unable to think of alternatives, to imagine a positive future, or to reach out to those most loved. Suicide is not a wish to be dead or to abandon us. The end that those who are suicidal seek is not of life itself, but of torturous emotional pain – in many cases the result of severe depression. When I and others look back on the lead-up to the death we grieve, we see clear signs of the desire for life.

Today I know what I didn't know then, which is that asking someone you're worried about directly about suicidal thoughts or plans – the thing we might most fear asking – is the safest thing to do. I know that for many here, from grief and the struggle to understand comes the conviction that suicide is not inevitable, that lives can be saved, that individually and collectively we can be attentive to the needs of those in pain, especially the many who suffer grievous emotional injury but are unable themselves to see their suffering as treatable and do everything in their power to avoid a stigmatizing diagnosis of mental illness, and so cannot or will not seek the help they desperately need. Many touched by suicide are now working with hope to make our communities and institutions more alert to those who are vulnerable.

And I think many living with loss know of nothing more powerful, as a force for healing, both for those who are vulnerable and for those who are bereaved than to share with others and to know that we are not alone. And that is the purpose of this service.

Bewilderment (2016)

Since one utterly devastating afternoon six years ago when I learned of my own son's death, this country has lost more than 37,000 people to suicide. We who are gathered here are just a few among the hundreds of thousands whose lives have been shaken to the core by suicide. We are weighed with the sorrow, the grief and the inner turmoil that suicide and its contemplation brings; and we are here for the solace that togetherness can provide when we face tragedy that's not just unfathomable, but unspeakable, and greatly stigmatized in our society.

We've just heard the beautifully sung words, hope, faith, life, love; but each of us affected by suicide – parents, children, sisters, brothers, friends, colleagues and those facing a darkness within – knows what it means for these pillars of survival to be ripped away. After my beloved Jake killed himself, I had to face the truth that the love of a father was not enough to recover a self-worth stripped by depressive illness, that inner pain could overwhelm the impulse for life itself, that faith or trust in the world or the future could be radically undermined and that there exists a dreadful state of hopelessness – changeless despair, moving from pain to pain in a world 'airless and without exits'[1] – a state of mind that makes positive thought or reaching out simply impossible.

What shocks many is that the thoughts of death that this brought to those like Jake were hidden. How many of us would say, 'We had no idea', 'We didn't understand the desperation', 'He was getting better'? The wish to die is revealed to the bereaved as a terrible secret, hidden from family and friends, perhaps by extraordinary effort, itself contributing to suicidal exhaustion. Nothing is more haunting than the later

---

1 Al Alvarez, 2002, *The Savage God: A Study of Suicide*, London: Bloomsbury, p. 293 (1971, Weidenfeld & Nicholson).

realization that the person we love had already disengaged from the world of the living.

Perhaps like others here, my own love and hope in life and trust that things would improve meant that I simply couldn't understand the darkness and danger into which my dear Jake had fallen. I didn't know how to read the signs that there were; signs that did not warn. And that's why love brings unbearable guilt to the bereaved by suicide. As survivors we ask the guilt-drenched 'what-ifs', 'if onlys', and 'what could I have done?', perhaps at some level trying to undo what cannot be undone.

But for many, knowing that the worst can happen also brings a new vigilance; a sensitivity and openness to others, an awareness of the fragility of life that is always lived with hidden layers. And so we understand now that there is no way to know the risk facing another except by breaking though the concealment and daring to ask someone if they have thoughts of suicide.

We have all learned bitterly from suicide about the destructiveness of the human mind, but also that those who are intensely suicidal may be in that state for a short period of time. And many who have been pulled back from the edge are unbelievably grateful for the second chance they have been given. Often those who are suicidal do not want to die, but rather experience emotional pain beyond the threshold of what is tolerable. They want to feel better but do not know how, and see no means to rebuild selves that have fallen apart, and cannot ask for help.

But herein is also hope that comes from knowledge that suicide is not inevitable. Other lives can continue. There are no easy solutions, but we can reorganize the way we think and listen, arrange education, health services and crisis support to make our families, our communities, our country and our world safer from suicide.

So, during this short service, we stand together to acknowledge the bewilderment of suicide and its painful aftermath and to remember how crucial we are to each other.

Relatedness (2017)

We are gathered here because we are all affected by the tragedy of suicide – the word itself conveys the worst fears and anxieties in ourselves and in our society, and for this reason is so often unspeakable.

'Time to Talk' is especially for those of us isolated by the fear and misunderstanding surrounding suicide, both those who have faced the limits of human forbearance and know what it means to feel life is unliveable, and those who are survivors of tragic loss to suicide. Thank you all for being here. We acknowledge the experience of loss and the guilt that blocks the path to self-care; we look forward to finding the strength to endure, to healing and finding purpose, and to helping ourselves out of solitude, especially through reaching out to one another; we look, that is, to human love.

Love, it seems to me, is why suicide is so difficult and so utterly painful. Love is that human condition which means that we none of us own ourselves. We have, and are, shared selves. Suicide is an act within this world of relatedness, often in response to unbearable emotional pain rather than the desire to abandon us, that tears apart and contradicts what is essential to our very being.

When, seven years ago, my son Jake took his own life, I remember feeling that I had become a part-person, a half-person – one arm, one leg, half a body, incomplete, something fundamentally missing. Although I stretched with all my being, suicide placed my son beyond reach, but not his pain. When someone dies by suicide, those bound by love often experience a shadow of the pain and anxiety that preceded the death they grieve, and the guilt. Guilt, because in the search to understand *why*, we are so connected that we make ourselves the first accused.

As we continue our search for answers, 'Suicide saddens the past [at the same time as it] abolishes the future', as Simon Critchley puts it. But suicide cannot offer reasons because, he writes, 'Reason [itself] runs headlong into one last, long tunnel with no exit.'[2] I do not believe that my son Jake wanted oblivion. His passion for life, his optimism and energy were just too great. And how could death be a solution for any problem that is within life?

Understanding why he, and so many like him facing incomprehensible pain and despair, felt that to die was the only solution, and endeavouring to make other solutions more thinkable and accessible for those in this desperate state, is the challenge we all face. This is a challenge made so much harder by the stigma and silence that allows suicide as an option to grow in the dark corners of tormented and isolated minds. This perilous silence has to be broken. It really is 'time to talk about it'.

As I sat holding my son, worried sick by his rapid onset severe depression, I did not know what I know now – and what every parent, sibling, friend, bartender, or taxi driver should know – which is that if you are

---

2 Simon Critchley, 2015, *Notes on Suicide*, London: Fitzcarraldo Editions, p. 66, p. 42.

worried about someone, the safest thing to do is, with empathy, to ask about thoughts of suicide. At the time, the idea of suicide was wrapped up in such fear and stigma as to be unthinkable; the conversation that I now wish I'd had was emotionally beyond reach. But such conversations are the frontline of prevention, reaching into suicidal isolation.

The hope that comes with this Time to Talk service is that those who we have lost will come to live in our hearts, forever returned as part of us, that standing together as people with lost parts, we can gain healing and wholeness; and that by understanding what it means to face death, we can nurture the wish to live.

Responsibility (2018)

I know that for some of us, it has not been easy to come here. I mean the pain of sitting with the effects of suicide in our lives. And yet here we are, surrounded by mutual understanding that does not even need words, and from which I hope you will find comfort. As usual, this service has the shape of a journey as we first reflect on loss in our lives, second, acknowledge the particular hardness of grief surrounding suicide that is like a journey through a deep valley, and finally to think about what we have found on that journey that gives us strength and hope.

Profound and irrecoverable loss may be at the heart of what leads to the tragedy of suicide – loss in its many terrible forms: loss of a person, loss of a relationship or a home, loss of a vision, of a destiny or of hope, the loss of honour, loss that produces unbearable emotional pain, that weighs heavier than life itself. And most of us are here because we live with a loss that seems, at times, unbearable. We have lost someone dear to us by their death, but we have also, by their suicide, lost them in another way, because mostly we cannot really answer the question *why* they have gone.

As I struggle to recover in my mind the son I so loved untainted by suicide; as I strive not to lose his whole person, I need explanations for this death that lie beyond him and his choices: his depressive illness, the effects of serotonin metabolism, the unseen work of genetics, unresolved grief, perfectionism, impulsivity or any other unknown figure or mad agent of death that took control of, and took away, my darling son. And suicide is so couched in this feared otherness that some of us feel we have lost part of ourselves, our identity, our role in society – perhaps as parent, or sibling or son or daughter, friend or colleague. Much of the judgement we feel may be in our own minds (a projection); but it comes from our society.

Why is our journey with suicide grief so hard? For one thing, the sorrow and regret we have become laden with guilt, as so often we take responsibility for something over which we had no control. Of the many spinning wheels that come to be aligned to produce a tragic death by suicide, we home in on the segment that shouts, 'I could have done something!' Responsibility is a matter of relational closeness; love makes us responsible.

Those who have left us by their own hand stay close. Their tragedy is in the places and the times of our everyday lives; the cracks, crevices and crossings through which they slip into our hearts, our fears, our phobias. We are changed by this journey with grief. A loss to suicide simply cannot be absorbed into everyday life. We who carry the emotional burden of suicide often find that our way of being in the social world is changed: there are avoidances, concealments, withdrawals and silences, because there are no words. Such is the valley.

But as we journey, we do find words to fill wordless pain. We find ways to talk and make some sense of what makes no sense; we discover our own stories. A narrative about my son's death that allows me to reinvest in life, to recover my place in society; and for my son to live untroubled in my heart. Many people living with suicide find new qualities in themselves, and new concerns. Suicide is a commission to change our world and prevent further suicides. We have a faithfulness to the tragic event that 'can also be "fated" – it simply happens to you and you cannot make it unhappen. You actively devote yourself to it, this part of you that you cannot part from.'[3] This does not happen alone. Finding others has been so important to living with my loss and turning it outwards. Friends, family but especially others who share the loss to suicide – in support groups, for example – help me find a language for suicide bereavement. I find the power of such fellowship extraordinary. We offer mutual recognition, borrow fragments of each other's stories with which to build our own and act in the world. Loss is born and hope discovered with others.

On this day, the 3rd March, the date on which my son Jake ended his life eight years ago, I want to say thank you to everyone – and there are so many – who through your own burden of loss have helped me carry mine.

---

3 T. Kuan, 2017, 'The Problem of Moral Luck, Anthropologically Speaking', *Anthropological Theory* 17 (1), pp. 30–59, p. 54.

Time (2019)

This Time to Talk service offers a moment of reflection, solidarity and hope in our journeys of grief, and recovery. And we are at different stages, and on different journeys. Thank you for the power of shared presence in the face of pain and loss, and the care that this shows. I know that for many being here is not easy.

The two words 'time' and 'talk' are, for me, central to the journey of life after suicide. Let me start with time. For some of us, the journey to this point began with a catastrophe so abrupt and brutal that time itself was ruptured. We may have wondered, as I did, how it was that the earth continued turning on its axis; because for me it didn't seem to. The poet Denise Riley knows how grief stops time, when movement, life, water and sky, just freeze, and 'All that should flow is sealed, is poised in implacable stillness.'[4]

When my son Jake died by his own hand, he seemed to be a bird in flight, 'halted in free-fall' never reaching the love that stretched out my arms to catch and to hold him. Thereafter, like others, I shared Riley's experience of living in arrested time, 'life without its flow' an altered condition of life lifted clean out of habitual time.[5] I bargained with time. In my repeating dreams, and through guilt-ridden rumination, I relived steps in time, again and again. In the emotional force of self-blame and taking responsibility for what could not be controlled, I tried to force time backwards, to unhappen what had, unbelievably, happened.

If time was paralysed, so was talk. There is no language in the aftermath of death by suicide; no words that explain; only an insurgent, croaking question, why? A characteristic of trauma is that verbal sense-making is near impossible. The event is too enormous and terrible to take in. And those who live with the effects of suicide – those who suffer loss or who in crisis feel the wish to die – know how our society extends this silence around suicide to keep it unspeakable.

The first part of this service speaks to what is lost with suicide. But we will journey through a valley – the valley of the shadow of death, for sure – towards hope, perhaps a re-entry into time, and recovery of talk and of voice. Recovering ourselves in ordinary time is not easy when a

---

4 Denise Riley, 2016, 'A Part Song' in *Say Something Back*, London: Picador, p. 13.
5 Denise Riley, 2012, *Life Lived, Without its Flow*, London: Capsule Editions, p. 10.

future life has been erased, and when the death by suicide of the ones we mourn seeps into and steals our memories of them, rewriting their past, thieving innocence and joy from the boyhood photographs of my darling Jake.

I do not believe that suicide loss can ever be absorbed into ordinary time or my life's trajectory. I won't lose the sense of being thrown into a different time. We do not 'get over it': the work of time on this bereavement is erratic and unpredictable. This grief has its own time. But I *have* found, and learned from others, a way to be present again in time, to live, to grow, to plan, to anticipate, to celebrate, to hope, to try to bring change. And I have found a way – also guided by fellow travellers – to talk about suicide and loss, and through talking, to connect, and to act as part of a community. And it is with others – in family, with friends, support groups, in charities, or the health service – that by talking about suicide, while embracing life with its flow in time, we have begun to lift the silence around suicide; the silence that is a real danger to those in crisis and in grief.

That's why it matters to have and to be in this Time to Talk.

Connection (2020)

It is ten years since I lost my son Jake to suicide. We know that the journey of grief following suicide is long, different from other kinds of bereavement, and individual. But we also know that our journeys can be shared so that we are not alone.

At the moment, the threat of a new virus has brought fear of human contact, talk of obligatory social distance, self-isolation, seclusion, quarantine … The response to a rapidly spreading virus to which we have no immunity is, of course sensible and necessary. Suicide is not an infectious disease and yet it brings social avoidance, stigma, distance, isolation and psychological handwashing in its aftermath.

Experts do talk about 'suicide contagion', by which they mean that closeness and affinity with someone who has taken their own life can increase vulnerability to suicide – in particular, as an unthinkable course of action becomes *thinkable*. And for this reason, *how* we talk about suicide, and how the media report a tragic death, matters. But in other ways, in our society we treat suicide as a kind of contagion surrounded with fear and anxiety in a manner that is unhelpful in the distancing and disconnection this creates.

We may fear to ask if someone is feeling like ending their life because what will we do if they say 'yes'? There is a fear of caring. In healthcare settings, the procedural risk assessments, referrals and protocols may seem to those in extreme distress like the donning of surgical gloves and facemasks to ensure clinical distance, protection against emotional connection with their distress.

Those of us bereaved by suicide may also experience the impulse in others to withdraw from such dark pain. Many will know how the mention of suicide or disclosure of such tragic loss may seem to infect a room, creating awkwardness or distance. Suicide is 'contagious' because it is 'carried in the fear and lack of connectedness that follows from it' [Ruth Kloocke's talk in this book]. Suicide has no infectious causal agent. At the heart of any tragic death by suicide is something unknown and profoundly unknowable. But not uncommonly, the search for answers looks for causes, hunts for responsibility, and often brings feelings of guilt and self-blame to those closest to the one who has died. And fears of responsibility and blame can fuel disconnection, fear and distance around those in suicidal distress or those who are bereaved. It would be better if we could embrace responsibility for one another. As has been said, in relation to suicide, everyone is responsible, and no one is to blame.

I know suicide as the ultimate departure and disconnection; that of my beloved son from myself. I also know that the response to suicide – to suicidal crisis and suicidal loss – has to be connection. The responses to suicidal crisis that work are those that enable connection, often in the form of being present, listening and caring that overcomes the impulse to get rid of, or escape from, another person's pain. And the comfort we may have from mutual presence now, connected through painful sorrow, accepted and understood, might give relief from the awkwardness that suicide brings. Perhaps I, we, can for a moment set aside the heavy self-protecting cloak that we put on to cover the pain of suicide when out in the world.

Grief is born of love and many of us, as we come here, draw on deep individual wells of sadness, loss and unknowing. By being here, we demonstrate that these wells also connect and that our experiences, though different, are shared. The isolation of suicide meets the impulse to connect and recover what is core to our humanity. For me, deepening human connection is the only response to suicide – to journey from lostness, through the valley of the shadow of death, to find and be found by others.

Love beyond death (2022)

Coming here may have been difficult for you, because facing suicide is difficult. So much in our society recoils from speaking of suicide. This is what brings loneliness and isolation to those who feel suicidal, as well as to those in grief after suicide. That's why we're here, today: to know we are not alone.

I've discovered that a mutual empathy brings together those who have experienced being suicidal and those experiencing the trauma of loss through suicide. Indeed, in the turmoil of sudden and traumatic loss, many bereaved by suicide have a powerful sense in themselves of the overwhelming pain and the loneliness that made the person they loved wish to die. I know I felt a shadow of his pain after the death of my son Jake 12 years ago.

Those are terrible moments of darkness, fragmentation (being scattered into pieces) and existential threat. These are also, commonly, moments of trauma which are without words or voice. We might say that those we love who killed themselves *acted out* what they could not put into words, what they could not speak, or tell. And this leaves us with the echoing question, why, why?

The aloneness and silence of suicide, and of its grief, is why we come together now in this service: to bring words, voices and music. We are meaning-making animals. Our very being depends on the sense we can make of life. Suicide throws everything into confusion. We are in disbelief. Suicide almost always comes as a sudden shocking event that nobody truly foresaw. Even if we knew of a loved one's despair, we never expected this to actually happen. But we often forget this. Consumed by our own sense of responsibility and guilt, we forget that we really didn't know what was going to happen.

I have realized something recently about what happened to me after Jake's death, which I think many share. Immediately I heard, I was so overwhelmed with disintegrating confusion that I couldn't think. But very quickly, I grasped for sense with a story that placed me at the controlling centre. It was on what I had or had not done that I ruminated with searing guilt. Guilt is the way we, I, cope with intolerable, suffocating powerlessness, as we try to take control over what is utterly beyond us – something that cannot unhappen, but cannot be accepted. It can be calming to blame oneself. Neuroscientists even tell us that we can be addicted to the feeling of guilt. But then beyond the almost unscalable mountain of my parental responsibility lay the field of others' fault –

the failures of attention and care. Self-blame, the blame of others, and the struggle against meaninglessness, are processes of grief after suicide. Sometimes, this grief we have for the way someone died, for suicide, can be so overpowering that it crowds out the quiet sadness of loss – maybe for years.

Last Monday, I was at the wedding of one of Jake's best friends. I was touched to be invited; in a way, I was representing him. I felt Jake's presence, and his absence, in my body. I knew that whatever he had done in his life, and wherever he had travelled, he would have been there at that exact time, at that wedding. As Jake came up in the speeches, and I witnessed the enduring impact he is having on young lives 12 years on, I felt the sadness of his absence; but something else too. The tears that came to me were for him, the wonderful person that he was, but not about his suicide. I could feel how he was loved and continued to matter deeply to his friends.

My journey of grief after suicide began with the bewilderment of death beyond the reach of love. At that wedding, and more often now, I feel love beyond death. What I have found is my son in my heart less shaped by his suicide. Wherever you are, I hope that in this service you find something to help you on your journey.

8

Steps Toward Faith

SAMUEL WELLS

The aftermath of suicide (2015)

Gentleness is an old-fashioned word. It used to be a way of talking about class and refinement, shrouded in terms like genteel, gentleman and gentility. But gentleness isn't an outdated virtue. Gentleness is perhaps the most important thing in talking about suicide. I want to describe what gentleness means and why it's so important.

To be affected by suicide is to be surrounded by enemies. The enemy of memory, sometimes; the enemy of fears; the enemy of isolation, and shame, and guilt and regret; the enemy of loss, failure, doubt – the unknown. It's not hard to feel powerless and out of control when it feels like there are so many enemies.

One of the most paradoxical of all the sayings in the Bible is, 'My strength is made perfect in weakness.' It's not the kind of thing alpha males say. But what it shows us is that the way to address our vulnerability, our fear and our self-destructiveness is not with some great show of strength. It's through making friends with our weakness. And the name for that is gentleness.

It's all very well to say, 'Be gentle with yourself.' But what does that mean? I'm going to suggest three things.

The first is silence. Silence can feel like a great enemy, because if you stop moving, or talking, or tuning in to some kind of gadget, then your mind can go into overdrive. But silence can become a friend if it turns from being a place of absence to a theatre of presence. Silence is for listening to the abundance of what's out there: birds that sing and tweet, breezes that stir and swing, a tiny, busy world of insects and creatures. Silence is for watching, paying attention to texture, depth, hidden beauty and delicate detail, wispy cloud, distant blue sky and intricate snowflake. Time, instead of being a threat or a diminishing commodity, becomes irrelevant. In silence, a minute or an hour are the same. In short, silence heals and reconnects because it takes you out of yourself, places you in a much larger, more wonderful and more elaborate universe. Silence stops being the interval between distractions and starts being the place of exhilarating, infinite discovery. It's a fruit of gentleness.

The second thing gentleness means is touch. Many of the feelings associated with suicide are violent, sudden ones. Gentleness embraces those feelings but issues in tender touch. Holding a person's hand says, 'I am here. This is good. You can trust me. I'm not going to run away. I'm not in any hurry. Your body, your life (whatever you might be feeling), your presence, your hand – it's good. I'm not going to grab it. I'm going to cherish it. Holding your hand, I can feel the mystery of your flesh, the blood coruscating in your veins, the warmth and softness and creativity of your fingers. These are mysterious and wondrous things. We were made for solidarity. We were made to stand by each other in times of distress and sorrow. No one is an island. Together we are a continent.' Those are the tender things touch teaches. They are the fruit of gentleness.

And then, when you've made a foundation of silence and touch, you can begin to try words. In the absence of silence and touch, words can seem disembodied, arbitrary, meaningless. But if you've made friends with silence and trusted yourself to find good ways to touch, words don't have to do too much work. Actions have already spoken.

Understanding is already there. Words can be the icing, and not the cake. They may be things you've never said before, things you think may shock the listener, or even yourself, things you're not proud of, things that may not make a lot of sense. Words are faltering attempts to give feelings and images and ideas a name. If they're surrounded by silence and touch, those words usually come out very gently. Harsh words hurt. Gentle words heal.

Suicide is overwhelming because it brings together so many of the terrifying things about existence. If you've considered it, worried about a loved one who seems close to it, or have been hurt by bereavement through it, it may seem that happiness is way out of reach. Perhaps it is. But the truth is, happiness is seldom found by people who go looking for it. It's only discovered on the way by people who are seeking something more important. Silence, touch and words are that something more important. They're the way God loves us. They're the way to show solidarity to one another. They're the way to dismantle the enemies that sometimes seem to surround us. They're the way to be gentle with ourselves. They're the way, slowly, carefully, cautiously, to learn to live again.

What hasn't changed (2016)

The experience of losing a loved one to suicide is a profound trauma. It can be years, decades maybe, before the wound becomes less raw, before you regain the trust that today won't bring such horror, before you can breathe without feeling your lungs incapable of taking in the air the world has to give you. And for those who've come close to taking their own life, there remains a lingering wound from what it's like to get into a place where suicide seems the only, even the right, step.

Such trauma reduces most of us to silence. And so today is a day for coming together and saying, perhaps in just a few words, those things we still know to be true, even when so much else feels fragile and tentative.

What things do we still know to be true? If you pick up a Bible, and open it around about the middle, you won't find yourself amid the parables and stories of Jesus. You'll land in the middle section of the book of Isaiah. You'll find yourself among the realities of what the people of Israel were experiencing in exile. They'd been invaded, Jerusalem destroyed, and they'd been carried off a thousand miles east to Babylon. They'd been through profound trauma. And in the forty-third chapter of Isaiah comes a moment of rock bottom, when they look at one another and look at God, and work out what they can know for certain.

And they settle on what are, for me, some of the most tender and cherished words, not just in the Bible, but anywhere. The people ponder their story, how they were created and liberated, how God walked with them and made sacrifices to be with them. And then come the vital words. It's the moment when you discover what's at the very heart of everything – why the Bible was written. It's the discovery that offers a gentle, tender way out of trauma, and a purpose to our existence. It's these twelve words: 'You are precious in my sight, and honoured, and I love you.'

Precious; honoured; loved. Everything we want to say to our cherished ones who've been taken from us. Everything we need to hear when we're in the slough of despond. Precious, honoured and loved. See how all three words count. On its own, 'precious' sounds fragile, like a china doll: it says, don't come too close, I can break. But with the second word, precious means much more. It says, 'I am of infinite value, I am unique, I am without compare.' On its own, 'honoured' sounds dry, dutiful, obligatory, somewhat soulless. But with the first word it says, 'I deserve respect, I have my own integrity, there's more to me than simply my relationship with you.'

Then we add the third word, 'loved'. On its own, love may not be such a great word. It can be a word of superficiality, manipulation, exaggeration, cliché – a word easily dismissed through over-familiarity. To be loved without being regarded as precious and without being honoured isn't actually all that nice. But when you are all three – precious, honoured and loved – then you've found the secret at the heart of all things. It's everything we want to say to those we miss so terribly. It's everything we need to hear when we're shrouded in a blanket of despair. Precious, honoured and loved.

I've never forgotten the night my father put the phone down and came upstairs ashen-faced after getting the news that the man he'd been brought up with, the man he thought of as a brother, had gone into the woods with a shotgun and not come back. I'd never seen him so sad. 'Philip,' he said, and shook his head, and no more words came out – but his face told the rest. And then he did something I never remember him doing before or after: he turned me towards him, put his hands on my shoulders, and looked straight at me. We were male and British, and I was just a child, and words were not the way we expressed what lay between us. But what he was saying, I now realize, was, 'You are precious, honoured and loved. Never forget it. I'm telling you now, because I never found a way to tell Philip. Make sure you tell those you need to tell, while you still can.'

My father bore the scar of that day for the rest of his life. Many people know what such a scar feels like. Today is a day, in the silence of our hearts, for saying gently, quietly, to those who chose to end their lives, 'You are precious, honoured and loved.' It's never too late to say it, to realize again how deeply we mean it, and to write those words into the eternal memory of the ones we have lost.

But it could be those words of Isaiah aren't so much the words you need to say as the words you need to hear. You've been through profound trauma. But three things haven't changed: you are precious. You are honoured. You are loved. Now. And forever.

Lion (2017)

We are tiny creatures in a boundless universe that has already lasted for billions of years; and we're constantly perched between the fear that our existence is meaningless and the joy that we exist at all. We can never pretend that we know all there is to know, yet we get glimpses that incline us to think that everything we don't know is in the same trajectory as what we do know.

In the 2016 film *Lion*, Saroo, on his first night at catering college in Melbourne, Australia, has such a moment. At dinner with his tutor group, he sees a plate of sweet jalebi that stops him in his tracks. Suddenly he's transported in his mind and heart and sensations back to a market in a small town in India, where, as a five-year-old child, he salivated at the sight of a similar plate that was way beyond what his family could afford. He tells his tutor group his story – how, with his older brother Guddu, they would steal coal from trains and use their wits to make money to keep themselves, their mother and their baby sister alive. One of these escapades went terribly wrong and Saroo found himself locked in a train that took him two days' journey from home. After living a dangerous existence in Kolkata, he was taken into an orphanage, from which he was adopted by an Australian couple.

The fascinated tutor group are full of clumsy questions and facile solutions. What they can't seem to do is empathize with the emotional place Saroo finds himself in. By recalling the memories of his childhood home and the deprivations of his family, he's lost the security of his adoptive family and the love that his adopting parents had folded around him. He gets into a confused tangle with his adoptive brother Mantosh, whose transition from India to Australia was much more painful, and who frequently lapses into fury, self-harm and drug binges. Saroo alternates between complex searches on Google Earth to try to locate a town a thousand miles from Kolkata where his family may still live, and inconsolable despair on perceiving the grief of his birth mother and brother and the impossibility of ever locating them from the evidence of his fragile memories. In this despair his relationship with his girlfriend Lucy, with his adoptive mother and father, and with his own self-care all disintegrate.

It's not hard to relate to the three women in this story. There's Saroo's birth mother Kamla, with her indescribable grief at her five-year-old son going missing, and no shred of a clue where he's been for 25 years. There's Saroo's adoptive mother Sue, who did whatever she could to give this apparently orphaned boy a loving chance in life. And there's Saroo's girlfriend, who has become close to him, only to see the relationship unravel because Saroo can't express the guilt, powerlessness, hurt and isolation he feels, and the unravelling of his identity he experiences as his memories cluster and his hopes of meeting his birth mother fade.

Many know what it's like to be Saroo, weighed down and imprisoned by feelings of despair, hopelessness, meaninglessness, guilt and self-rejection.

Then everything changes. Saroo finally finds it in himself to visit his adoptive mother Sue and express how sorry he is that she was infertile and couldn't have her own children, because he and his adoptive brother have turned out to have brought such grief and dysfunction into her life. Sue turns to him and says, 'I'm not infertile. Your father and I could have had our own children. We *chose* to have you.' Saroo is dumbfounded. He begins to realize he's got the whole story of his adoptive family wrong. Half of his despair was based on a false premise, an assumption that turned out to be groundless.

Then, after years of mental chaos, for the first time his Google searching lands on a geographical location that resonates with his memories of early childhood. The other half of his despair is ripe for reconfiguration too. In no time he's on a plane to India. What he discovers there isn't a perfect resolution to his story: there's sadness as well as joy. But his life is transformed from the paralysis of dismay to the energy of purpose. And his three key relationships can begin again. His final discovery is that his name never was Saroo. He'd always mispronounced it. It was really Sheru, the Hindi word for 'lion'. For the first time, he discovers who he really is.

Lion is a true story. It's a film about adoption and a film about cultural dislocation. But most of all it's a film about depression, and how a person from an apparently secure background can become isolated by assuming a story that's only one part of the truth, and dwelling on that story so much that it obscures all other insights and dismantles all close relationships. By the end of the film, Saroo hasn't unlocked a superficial happiness; but he has found a level of peace in which he is able to recognize how precious his relationships are and, like never before, to receive from those who love him so much. The key moment in the whole film is when he feels bold enough to seek out his adoptive mother Sue and test out his story with her – only to find he's misunderstood all along, and rooted his despair in a narrative that turns out to be largely untrue.

Depression is real. There's no doubt about that. But there can sometimes be a genuine way out. And that way out is often through discovering a much larger story than the one we thought we were in. The only way to find that story is to test what we thought we knew with someone who will take time to listen and engage and sometimes be able to show us that there's a larger picture, a picture that has so much more love in it than we had ever imagined. Saroo's life changed when he realized it was time to talk. Ours can too.

But there's one reality the film chooses not to dwell on. And that's the reality of Karmal, Saroo's birth mother. Many know what it's like to lose a child or close relative – constantly to search one's memory and one's conscience to identify if there was anything one could have done, in an effort to dispel the powerlessness of grief. The reunion between Saroo and Karmal is poignant viewing for those who've spent countless dark hours longing to see again a person they struggle to live without. That's an experience the movies shy away from; but a reality many know all too well. May our efforts be about encouraging those facing depression to enter a larger story, with a lot more love in it; but also about cherishing one another when the ending won't come right, and facing together the truths that the movies don't want to describe.

Time to talk (2018)

A few years ago I was asked to take the funeral of a woman whom I hadn't known but who had lived in the parish where I was vicar. It was a sad story because the woman, who was in her seventies, had had a particularly painful wasting disease. The pain had got so great that one night she had stepped out of bed, put on slippers and a dressing gown, let herself into the back garden, climbed the fence, walked into the local lake and drowned herself. I listened to her widower telling me the story. At the funeral I talked about the things we knew and the things we didn't know. I said we didn't know what anguish was going through her mind, but we did know how deeply she was loved and will be missed. I said we didn't know what could bring her to such despair, but we did know her life had been beautiful and those who knew her loved her and would always cherish what she'd meant to them.

A week after the funeral I paid a visit to the widower to see how he was doing and show him I was thinking of him. I was fully prepared for him to say how beautiful the funeral was and there was always a chance he might say how well I'd spoken. But he didn't. He looked straight at me, head still and unblinking, and said, 'What you said was completely wrong. You said we don't know what was going through her head when she got out of bed and walked down to the lake. That's not true. I know exactly what she was thinking. She'd tried before, and afterwards she told me what it was like. I know what she was thinking. I told you that when you came to see me last time. But you weren't listening, were you. Maybe you didn't want to listen.' He didn't say it in an angry way, but more in a weary voice, as if I was just one of a series of people who hadn't really listened, either to her or to him.

I learned something important that day, something that has stayed with me ever since. If something's awful for somebody else – if I'm in a conversation with a person who's considering suicide or so depressed they don't know how they can go on – my role is not to make things better. Not just because I can't, but for two other reasons. Reason one is that almost any attempt I make to suggest that things are actually OK and the person needn't be so miserable is almost bound to be superficial and trite, and by being so shallow will actually increase the isolation of the other person – which is a big part of what they're actually struggling with. Reason two is that my attempt to persuade may end up convincing myself and not my companion, making it all the more likely that I'll get fed up with my companion being so miserable, and in the end lose patience with them and walk away.

My role is not to make things better, because that leaves the person more isolated than before. Instead, my role is to stand beside them as they face the hardest things in their life, one of which may turn out to be their fear that they could get to such an isolated place that they might consider something awful and destructive. If it's awful, I don't say, 'Maybe it's not so bad.' I say, 'It seems very painful. I wonder which is the hardest part. Maybe you can try to put it into words so that I can share what's giving you so much pain to be thinking about on your own.' If you have a choice between giving someone false hope and giving them the truth, always give them the truth, because once they've realized that hope is false then they'll be worse off than before; but if they can name and face the truth, and realize they've not scared you away, and found that they're still here, then they may learn the path to life, which is, if you stay with the truth and walk through it then you can come out the other side of it and find you're still alive. And if you do that, you're on the other side of hell, and hell can't hurt you in the same way as before. And if your companion is still there, you know a love that's stronger than death. And when someone is looking straight at the truth, about themselves or about the universe and everything, the best thing you can do is to stay still and hold their gaze and not look away.

We're bound to ask the question about ourselves and our loved ones, 'Is love as strong as death?' And gathering together in the face of suicide is to answer, 'Yes. Stronger.' But we don't say it for people: we can only learn to say it for ourselves. Showing up together is a statement and a prayer that those most on our hearts, dead or alive, may come to know the truth of those words: 'Love is stronger than death.'

Gratitude (2019)

Not long ago I caught up with an old friend. I'd tried to get in touch a few times, without success. But finally, I was going to be in the town where she lives, so I practically broke the door down trying every route to tell her so. When we got together, she said, 'Sorry about the silence. I was off work for a few months with depression.'

It was a moment of real honesty, but of course I was eager to hear more. I knew the bare bones. The first marriage that unravelled; the second one that was a disaster from the word go. The frustrated career plans, after such success early on. The unsatisfactory job that got worse and worse from day one, and ended up being unachievable. But what I hadn't realized was the psychological toll. Inside she became a wretched mix of anger, regret and powerlessness, and started to seal herself off from her children, and not answer emails from people like me.

If I'd known what was going on, I'd have been really worried. But that's the point, as everyone who's encountered suicide knows. I didn't realize what was going on. Maybe partly because I didn't want to believe it. But mostly because she didn't want me to know. Didn't want me to know because she didn't think she was worth my time, anyone's time; and didn't want me to know because she'd got herself to a place where she didn't believe anyone would really get it, or could genuinely reach her.

What changed? Well, the first thing was she began to find a way to notice, to value, and then to enjoy the tiny details of her life. The big things seemed like they'd all gone wrong, and she was deeply, truly sad about that. So sad she couldn't put it into words. But somehow she managed to put the big things aside and start to appreciate the little things. She found these words: 'Enjoy the little things, for one day you may look back and realize they were the big things.' And she realized that they described the most recent few weeks of her life. The little things were the feeling of fresh cotton sheets on her bed, the joy of mid-morning coffee, the crisp air of a blue-sky winter day.

And then, as if she was graduating from one truth to another, she found these words: 'The more you express gratitude for what you have, the more likely you will have even more to express gratitude for.' She found the truth of those words. She was grateful for the food she ate for breakfast, for the mystery of bread, the texture of butter, the simple action of spreading one on the other. And slowly she became able to say, 'Despite all, my three daughters. They've turned out all right. I'm proud of them. I must have done something OK.'

Then she found some more words to cherish: 'There are only two ways to live your life. One is as though nothing is a miracle. The other is as though everything is a miracle.' She realized she'd changed from the first way to the second way. She'd come close to taking her own life. But now every tiny second began to seem like a gift and, yes, a miracle. Everything was a miracle. She'd once looked on the local park as pointless, because everything was pointless, empty, a charade and a cosmic joke. But when she started with the tiniest things – a leaf, a blade of grass, the rustle of leaves – she realized she couldn't create any of it – it was all gift – all miracle. Then she found some more words: 'Gratitude is happiness doubled by wonder.'

Gratitude is happiness doubled by wonder. It was as if she'd stumbled upon happiness while assuming it wasn't for the likes of her. And her route there was simple: gratitude. By noticing the tiniest things, she'd come to appreciate them; by appreciating them she'd started to be grateful for them. Quickly she became grateful for all the tiniest things, and there were so many tiny things she began to forget about the big things – until the little things became the big things.

Finally, she discovered these words. 'Some people grumble that roses have thorns; I am grateful that thorns have roses.' She realized those words expressed the change in her life. She said to me, 'More than anything, I just feel so lucky. I'm just so grateful.' It felt like she'd made the most important journey any of us can make in life. Now she had nothing to fear. The anger, the powerlessness, the bitterness were all beginning to ebb away. And the most amazing thing of all was this: she said, 'You know, if I hadn't had that time of depression, I'd never have learned those things. I know for some people it's a death sentence, the worst possible maze from which there's no escape. But for me, I'm starting to think it was actually the beginning of my life.'

Be gentle (2020)

'Look after yourself.' It's a strange expression. It's curious how it's become a common way of saying goodbye. It's almost uncomfortably pointing out that there may be no one actually looking after you, so saying, 'Don't forget to look after yourself, then.' I think it means, 'I care about you, and I wish I could be around to make your life better, so treat yourself the way I'd treat you.' But it doesn't *say* it. 'Take care.' There's another one. It's apparently saying, 'You live a reckless life, and you'd better watch out or one wrong move might be the last.' But I think it's trying to say, 'I wish I could take care of you, but I can't, so remember how I think about you and think that way about yourself.' It should be saying, 'Life's precious, treasure it.' But it sounds like. 'You're like a car that doesn't know where it's going.'

Here's a better one. 'Be gentle.' I like that one, because I like the person I am when I'm being gentle – and I like people being gentle with me. Today this church is full of people who have either come close to taking their own life, or been close to someone who has actually ended their own life. I want to say a few words about how we can be gentle with those in a precarious mental state, and how we can be gentle with one another when we're swathed in the grief, guilt, regret, isolation and powerlessness that come with suicide and loss.

It starts with stillness. Stillness says, 'I don't have anything better to do than be with you. You don't have to be interesting, clever, entertaining or cheerful. You don't have to say anything at all. I'm not here to judge you. I'm not here to make you change your mind. I'm not going to get bored, or angry, or impatient. I'm not here to fix you, or pretend everything's fine. I can see you're sad. I'm not making up stories about what's the matter with you. I just know that companionship is the best thing in life, and I'm here to give you that. I don't have a script for how this is supposed to go. I'm just here to say you're not alone.'

Then there's care. Care uses the senses. 'I can see your shoulders are hunched. It looks like you're feeling on edge.' 'I've heard you use the word "abandoned" two or three times. Is that something you've been feeling a lot?' 'You look frightened. Would you like me to hold your hand?'

Notice we haven't even used any words yet. But there'll be a time for words. Often we use words and actions as distractions. 'Can I get you some tea?' we say, when we don't like the way the conversation's going. 'Did you see the Liverpool result last night?' we ask, when we're trying to get our companion onto safe territory. But those aren't always the gentle words. The gentle words are ones like, 'Tell me more about that.' Or, 'That looked like a hard thing to say. I wonder if there are other things it's hard to say.' Or, 'I wonder what's the hardest thing right now.'

Let me tell you a secret. Other people are sent to us as a gift. We almost always find what they're struggling with is greater than what we're facing. And instead of that feeling like an added burden, it more often makes us feel liberated; like actually our stuff isn't quite so bad after all. People say to me, 'I'm sorry, I've taken up your time.' But I say, 'No, it's done me good listening to you. Thank you for trusting me.' And what I think, but don't say, is, 'I can feel a gratitude I've seldom felt, now that I know the solidarity of your suffering, and now I know I'm not alone.'

We have a choice in relationships. We can go all out with kindness and support, and end up feeling naive and worn out – maybe even used. Or we can go towards challenge and truthfulness, and end up feeling harsh and mean – maybe even heartless. But there's such a thing as gentle attention, which is somehow beyond either. Gentle attention is still – but alert. It sees – but doesn't judge. It touches – but doesn't control. It speaks – but only to encourage us to discover more ourselves.

I believe gentle attention is the way God sees us. We're told Jesus was full of grace and truth. That's what gentle attention is – full of grace and truth. Everyone associated with suicide is united by one thing – suffering. Suffering can't be fixed, changed, distracted from or answered. It can only be accompanied, with gentle attention. If we learn one thing from our suffering, it's the tender power of gentle attention. Be gentle.

Love is stronger than death (2022)

Suicide is the biggest taboo in our culture, because death is the stripping away of everything that matters. The loss of breath, of our body, of relationship, of consciousness, of memory, of hope, of identity, of capacity, of strength, of life, of love. To die at your own hand is all of these things, but with added pain. It's a fearful statement of the utter loss of confidence in life, and in love. And to those around you, even though almost never intended that way, it can be experienced as a profound and unanswerable form of rejection.

Death poses the most disturbing question of all. And that question is this. Is life, is this energy and activity and awareness and thought – is all this the most real thing? Or is there something, deep down, beneath it all, that is truer, more permanent, more eternal than life – something called ... nothing? It's the most troubling question, because if nothing is more real than this something, then everything around us is no more than a kind of long-term illusion, a perpetual mirage – which is here today, and perhaps tomorrow, but gone the next day, never to return. It does your head in. It makes you wonder if the reason people keep busy is to avoid ever thinking something like that. It makes you wonder what would become of any of us if we allowed ourselves to sit and think like that for a long time.

And it's this question that makes people create sacred buildings like this and attend momentous events. And the strange thing is, tucked away in a relatively obscure book in an unfindable section of the Old Testament, lies an answer. A challenging answer. Towards the end of the Song of Songs are the five words that address our deepest question. 'Love is strong as death.' Or some versions say, 'Love is stronger than death.' When all things are said and done, and death has done everything it can do, there's still love – fragile, maybe, battered, certainly, but abiding, nonetheless. Life is more than nothing. The central moment in the Christian faith is when a man went to die – a man who was utterly isolated. Deserted and betrayed by his friends. Apparently abandoned by God. Practically no one was there, besides people mocking him. He went to show that love is stronger than death.

The truth is, we, gathered here today, are in different places about how we hear those words. Some of us are feeling very painfully that love is not stronger than death – because this death, this terrible death, seems to have obliterated everything. Some of us are in a slightly different place, a place that has days of hope as well as days of despair; a place that says, tentatively, love is strong as death. The two are in a tussle that feels like it'll go on a long time. But others again are in a third place, inspired perhaps by the death of the abandoned one or perhaps inspired in other ways, but nonetheless ready to say, through tears and struggle, that however bleak suicide can be, however isolated, sad, forsaken and neglected a death can be, however much a person taking their own life can seem to nullify life and relationship and hope and everything, at the end of time, love is stronger than death. It's just five words. Love is stronger than death.

My point isn't about judgement. It's not about saying you've got to be in one of those three places. It's about the solidarity of us all standing together, whatever death has done to our sense of love or our ability to love. It's about putting a gentle embrace around everyone affected by suicide and finding something true together we couldn't find alone.

Love is strong as death. Some feel able to say, stronger. Some can't say that. Some can say that some days, but not others. The motivation of those who organize around the prevention of suicide is to create a space where those most profound feelings can be let out and shared and heard. This is the inspiration for people who work in mental health support; for those who create opportunities for people who feel they have nowhere to turn and that life is hopeless.

Love is strong as death. Maybe we can say, stronger. It's a mission statement for life. It's what we're saying by reaching out to a stranger and listening to their story. It's not something to shout. It's something to whisper. It's a way to live.

An influence immense; a loss unfathomable (2023)

Not long ago, a person I greatly admired, younger than me, ended her life. At the inquest, both her husband and her psychotherapist testified they had no idea something like this was coming. She was immaculately efficient, fiercely funny, highly disciplined, rigorously honest and universally loved. Within minutes of the news becoming known, people were searching for understanding, comprehension and consolation. I spent much of the rest of the day on Zoom with those who hoped I could offer some insight, explanation or comfort. I couldn't. I could only offer one thing: companionship. I wonder if many, perhaps most of us, who gathered in the face of suicide are likewise looking for understanding, comprehension or consolation. But the one thing I most hope we find is companionship.

The person I much admired was called Anna. I couldn't attend her funeral, but I scoured the words people had said about her to find the understanding, comprehension and consolation I couldn't conjure up for myself. One put it succinctly: 'Alongside a deep humility ... lay an incapacity to recognize in herself the gifts that others saw in her so abundantly, or to show towards herself anything like the depths of love that others felt for her.'

Those words actually helped me a lot. It wasn't blaming Anna: it was just naming the truth that she, for reasons no one seems to know, got into a place of having an inexplicably low opinion of herself. The same person said another beautiful thing: 'Dying so young, she leaves an influence as immense as her loss is now unfathomable.' That summed up her legacy perfectly.

Another friend said a similar thing differently: 'The extravagant and unconditional love of God she showed to others, she sometimes found harder to see belonged to her too. Her story about herself was sometimes different from the one we gratefully related. ... Those who got close to her will recognize this fragility in her. We loved her for it, but she doubted it was loveable.'

Some time later, this is what I've learned from the loss of Anna. I've learned again how fragile and precious life is, and how we do well to cherish those we care about and tell them what they mean to us while we have the chance. I've learned that you can never fully know what's in another person's heart and soul. I've learned how a person's words about love, about life, about God, about hope, can mask their most profound doubts about everything. I've learned how the immense good and beauty a person can offer in their life is not lessened by the last thing they did. I've learned that there are some questions in life to which no one has the answer, and to which, however much we ask, we'll never receive an adequate reply.

But most of all, I've learned what I found that first evening after the news about Anna broke: the solidarity of companionship. Anna created a community, even after her death: all who admired her found through her a language to express what they most valued in life. They lost her, but in a paradoxical way, they gained each other. And that points to something important about gathering in the face of suicide. This is a community brought together by tragedy and near-tragedy. Everyone has chosen not to seek solace alone, but to find understanding, comprehension and consolation in companionship. Insight may be elusive; explanations may never be forthcoming; sadness may never end. But companionship is a precious gift, maybe the most precious of all. Answers may be hard to find; but perhaps the best place to look is one another.

The solidarity of grief (2024)

I want to tell you about a conversation that changed my life. 7 September 2024 would have been my mother's 94th birthday: but it wasn't, because 40 years before that, she died after a 13-year journey with cancer. I was 18 and bewildered; coming to terms with a terminal illness that goes on forever was one thing, but the transfer to grief and loss was another.

To make sense of it, I reached out to my schoolfriends. But how could they understand? Yet one of them did. I got news about Steve. I hadn't seen him for a few months, but I took courage and called. 'I heard about your mum,' I said. 'Yeah,' he grunted. 'I wondered if you'd like to meet for a drink,' I ventured. 'Why not?' he replied.

He told me how one morning his mother sent his dad off to work, gave him a hug, and then set off from her house in Bristol, my hometown. But that morning she didn't go to work. Instead, she walked half a mile, laid down her briefcase, and jumped to her death from Clifton Suspension Bridge. He said the words matter-of-factly. I was in awe of how he held it together. I said, 'I had no idea your mum was so ill.' He said, 'We didn't talk about it.'

Then I told him my story. Of how my mother told me when I was five that she might not come home. And again when I was nine. And again when I was 15, though with more finality this time. And how she still did. Until eventually, painfully and agonizingly, it was over. He said, 'I had no idea your mum was so ill.' I said, 'We didn't talk about it.'

I reflected, 'So, they're two very different stories.' And then Steve said words I would never forget, even today, 40 years on. 'But don't you see – they're not different stories. Your mum died of a terminal illness. My mum did too. She lived on the edge, on the membrane between life and death. For years we wondered if we'd get a phone call. Finally we did. Your mum's death and mine may look very different. But they both hovered for years between death and life – and finally gave in.'

I was awestruck. I still am. An 18-year-old boy with such clarity and insight. Somehow he brought the unspeakable into our lived reality, and made it something we could speak about with what I would now call the solidarity of grief. We found something with each other that night that gave us both meaning and truth.

And it's that same something that provides the reason why it's good to gather in the face of suicide. We come together with different stories. We each have unique pain and isolating grief. But in surprising ways we have the same story. A story of a powerlessness we all share. A story of an emptiness that feels like it will never resolve. Yet, as we search for meaning and truth, we find ourselves together. And we're grateful for one another, because we find something surprising, profound and transformational.

It might not be faith; it might not yet be hope; it might not be meaning, truth or consolation. But what it is, is the soil out of which some or all of those things may eventually grow. It's a human experience chiselled in adversity and fostered in community. It's what we call solidarity: the solidarity of grief.

Part Three

9

Faith in the Face of Suicide

SAMUEL WELLS

In this chapter I'm seeking to describe suicide from the perspective of the Christian faith. I will pay attention to the viewpoints of other faiths, and I recognize that not all Christians share the perspective I outline here. But such a chapter belongs in this book because it seeks to portray the kind of Christian faith that underlies the annual service that led to this book being written. The annual service is a collation of perspectives including spiritual and secular; this chapter addresses the point of view that places the whole issue within the embrace of the God of Jesus Christ.

The gift of life

To say life is fundamentally a *gift* is to recognize that none of us chose to be born; no one could make themselves exist by deciding to come to be. Thus, that we each exist is a miracle and a mystery, and a daily source of wonder and gratitude. Life is also a *trust*. It exists in a network of story and community: we dwell in relationship with those who brought us into the world, those with whom we are raised, with whom we work, relax, abide, gather for festivals, share heritage, maintain convictions, enjoy fruits – in other words, those who will miss us when we're gone.

But to say life is a gift and a trust is also to say what life is not. Life is not a *right*. It's not a quasi-possession, something we're entitled to and can simply dispose of when surplus to requirements. It's not something whose pursuit is subject to our independent judgement alone. We may not welcome others' judgements about how we determine the course of our lives – particularly when we haven't sought their opinions – but the constant evaluation of and speculation about one another's options and choices are part of the ineradicable fabric of life. Meanwhile, neither is life a *duty*. To say none of us chose to be born also means none of us is inherently suited to the challenges and responsibilities life entails. In some circumstances those obstacles can be or feel insurmountable, or the assaults something we feel incapable of withstanding. Finding ourselves in such a situation is a matter not for blame but compassion. It's a condition in which any or all might find themselves; and in which some certainly do. That's not due to moral failure; but more like being afflicted by an illness.

When a person takes their own life, all four of these understandings come into play. Perhaps the initial and most intense is the second one: the fact is, in most cases, the people close by – parents, spouse, siblings, children, friends, colleagues, neighbours – feel an immense and limitless sense of loss, horror and dismay. The web of *trust* has been broken. The membrane by which we each hold ourselves in companionship, within which we hope that our love for one another will never let us go – this membrane has been pierced, and it can be as if the whole substructure of our lives is suddenly compromised: nothing is now certain or reliable, all is in flux. An extreme version of this reaction plunges us into guilt. To feel guilty in the face of suicide is to linger over things I should have said, kindness I could have expressed, efforts I should have gone to – even genes I shouldn't have passed on – that could have made all the difference; might, just possibly, have averted this catastrophe. But such guilt is to concentrate all trust – the web of relationships and understandings that underpin our well-being – onto oneself. It's entirely understandable in a condition of utter and agonizing powerlessness. But it's almost never justified or accurate. Yet trust *has* been broken. And life feels indescribably more fragile as a result. It's common for a person contemplating taking their own life to imagine that life would be easier for those around them should they no longer be alive. But few things hurt loved ones more than to think that their love was so misunderstood or overlooked, because such breaches the fabric of trust at its most tender point. Trust is the convention by which we overcome what would otherwise be utter isolation; and it's that sense of utter isolation that inclines us to suppose others would not miss us.

The next understanding that might come into play is the third, *right*. It may seem a debatable exercise of freedom, but to take one's life is undeniably an exercise of freedom. We may have made a mistake in our culture to make individual choice the highest social good; but it's difficult to imagine a culture in which taking one's life were not something one actually had the freedom to do. Even in our lowest moments of grief and despair, few of us would question that the person whose life we grieve should not have had the freedom to take their life at the point they had resolved to do so. The trouble is, this freedom, like all social goods, is not an end in itself. We may have the right to do something – and we may fiercely defend another person's right to do it – but that does not in itself make it a good thing to do. When we say to someone we love, 'You belong to me,' we know we're half joking; but we're still saying something very important. When we take on significant relationships – marriage, parenthood, responsibility for employees or institutions or another's well-being – we're in the tender areas of connections that can't be commodified or idly severed. If we drop them, they break. There may not be a law against doing so: but our actions still have consequences. Which demonstrates how unhelpful the language of 'right to life' can be: because it pares the issue down to individual choice, which ignores the network of relationships by which our lives are in practice constituted, and which resurface like a shock-wave when news of a suicide permeates a community.

In our anger, much of it driven by utter powerlessness, in the face of the suicide of one we love, we can sometimes turn to the fourth understanding – *duty*. It's a short journey from recognizing that being a parent, sibling, child, colleague, friend incurs a degree of trust to insisting it demands a level of duty. This is the moment when we're tempted to transfer the sense of guilt from ourselves, at having failed to prevent the person from determining to take their life, to the person themselves for having failed to appreciate the true worth of their life, the quality of the relationships they truly had and the devastation they leave behind. We can find ourselves torn between our compassion for the true despair in which our loved one found themselves, and our dismay at the damage caused by their death and the impulse to hold someone accountable. What was once a taboo on condoning a suicide has now almost completely reversed and been replaced by a taboo on any expression of anger towards the person who has left such a trail of emotional (and sometimes practical) wreckage after their death. Such anger is a natural and not uncommon stage in any process of grief: we may feel fury towards a person who has died and left us bereft in almost any circumstances – illness or accident. But deep down, we don't want people close to us to continue to exist out of duty alone when all other will to live has gone. Duty may be a vocation, but it's misused when we turn it into a weapon.

A longer period of reflection in the face of suicide may yield contemplation of the notion of *gift*. It's in the nature of a gift that we didn't choose to receive it and we can't determine its nature. The gift of life does not come in a form we'd select from a dropdown menu. Many of those whose stories are told in this book found themselves afflicted by mental illness of a kind such that their sense of the world and themselves became distorted. In some cases they changed from lively and outgoing to brooding and morose. In other cases they developed a side to their character that had never previously emerged – a side that took them to a dark, depressed and bleak place. They were, as we put it, 'not in their right mind'. What this is saying is that the gift of life – for which they had not asked, and which came in a form they had not chosen – had become one it was impossible for them to continue to receive: so much so that, under a cloud short or long, once or repeatedly, they found the burden of life too heavy to bear. When we see a person in a train station struggling with their luggage, our instinct is to offer or find help. But some luggage one can only carry oneself (or so it can seem, for short, long or indefinite periods); and some luggage is invisible to the observer, however intimate. When one is full of gratitude for the unsought and undeserved gift of life, it can be the very best feeling in the world; when one cannot deal with the impossible and relentless demand of continuing to exist, it can seem like the very worst thing in the world – and for some people, sometimes, it's so intolerable there's only one way out.

The purpose of God

There is a somewhat narrow view of what Christianity is about that contrasts with a rather broader view that sets the story of God in a wider perspective. The trouble is that the narrow view is widespread, and sinks deep into people's most tender areas of anxiety and guilt, and is difficult to eradicate and heal. But that doesn't necessarily make it true.

The narrow view is that humankind is lodged in a predicament with two kinds of jeopardy: profound sin that leaves us in a condition of guilt, facing judgement and potential punishment; and inevitable death due to inherent mortality, leaving us in a condition of transience, facing oblivion or obliteration. Jesus comes to overcome sin by providing a degree of suffering that offers sufficient sacrifice to make atonement; and to transcend death by emerging from the tomb in resurrection and thus making available to us eternal life. We access these two gifts, the forgiveness of sins and everlasting life, by believing in Jesus and keeping a set of rules that demonstrate our gratitude and obedience to God. It is sometimes (though not always) taken that suicide, by not cherishing the gift of life, is a transgression of this gratitude and obedience and thus a sin – even, according to some accounts, a sin of such magnitude that it imperils our receipt of forgiveness and eternal life.

The broader view is that the universe was created for God to be in relationship with humankind in Christ. Thus the Trinity of Father, Son and Holy Spirit is itself a relationship, and, accordingly, that precious quality of relationship is the reason for creation, the nature of the incarnation – God coming among us in Jesus – and the character of eternal life. Jesus didn't come to fix the guilt-and-mortality-problem – he came to embody the way in which God being with us is the central truth beyond and within all things. Our eternal life with God was never in danger – because God has no purpose to throw away that which has been created for relationship. Nothing is predetermined except that God should come to be with us in Christ and this shall show us what life with God eternally will be like. Our relationship with God could not be predetermined because every genuine relationship matures through the experience of surprise and setback. It can't be imposed or scripted. In this sense, suicide is a recognition that we sometimes find true, profound, wondrous and transformative relationship with God and one another elusive, and that, even though we do sense such relationship, the burdens of existence can sometimes prove intolerable. This is not our fault, or something for which we will be held temporarily or eternally responsible; it is a profound and genuine perception of some people in some circumstances. It is no more a reason for blaming those people than it is a pretext for upending our whole structure of conviction about everyone and everything.

One might think the narrow view is found in the Bible and the broader view has emerged on modern reflection. But in fact the two views exist side by side in the Bible and have continued to do so throughout the history of Christianity. The same is true for views about suicide. It's not the case that the Bible condemns it or that it has always universally been viewed negatively in Christian history.

Nowhere does the Bible explicitly and specifically condemn suicide. There are seven accounts of individuals taking their own life across the Old and New Testaments. Three of these follow the humiliation of defeat – Abimelech (Judges 9.52–54), Zimri (1 Kings 16.18) and Saul (1 Samuel 31.1–6; 1 Chronicles 10.1–6; Saul's armour-bearer also takes his own life). Two follow the recognition of, and consequent shame, guilt and regret, of betrayal – Ahithophel (2 Samuel 17.23) and Judas (Matthew 27.3–5). Samson kills himself along with 3,000 others in Gaza, in the first example of a 'suicide bombing' (Judges 16.30). None of these stories are accompanied by the narrator's censure. Indeed, all of them come within the notion of a noble death as respected in the ancient world, and in the case of Samson, the narrator suggests God gave him the strength to kill more in his death than he had in his life.

The Bible has little notion of psychological or psychiatric conditions that could lead a person to consider taking their own life. It does not speak of biochemical issues or specific emotional states. Nonetheless it does refer to situations we today would regard as that of depression or trauma. We are told that Solomon 'hated life' (Ecclesiastes 2.17), that Elijah was so frightened and desperate he asked God to take his life (1 Kings 19.4) and that Paul despaired of life itself (2 Corinthians 1.8). Thus, contemplating suicide is something people have done in all times and circumstances. It is not a sign that they have no faith or that they are in some sense especially flawed or have strayed from an honest path: it is an affliction that can come upon almost anyone through adverse circumstances or medical or biochemical conditions.

The aftermath of suicide can be devastating for loved ones and wider communities. It's understandable that, in seeking to preserve a person's well-being and prevent such damage to their close and wider circles, the Church has at different times placed a prohibition on suicide, and spoken in harsh terms about the fate of those who take their own life. This was an attitude that was reflected in British law: suicide was only decriminalized in England and Wales in 1961 (it had never been illegal in Scotland). But such a stance was misguided. It only increased the shame, horror and taboo around suicide, thus only exacerbating the pain and grief involved. And it was not founded on a careful reading of Scripture or profound understanding of the heart of God.

God is not fundamentally in the business of fixing our problems or demanding we live upright, uncomplicated lives. God longs to be in relationship with us – and every relationship undergoes challenges and struggles. Sometimes it is out of such adversities that even deeper relationship can grow. Suffering is never the purpose of God – but God's purpose can sometimes emerge out of, or be visible amid, times of hardship in a way it might not have otherwise been apparent or tangible. That purpose isn't for comfort and idle leisure – it's for something far more profound – for true relationship forged through dwelling and striving together in sorrow and in joy. That relationship does not end in death – but it is swept up into something more profound and more permanent. Thus suicide loses its most agonizing and most acute power – that of having the last word.

Here is a summary of views on suicide from other faith traditions, in their own words, beginning with Islam.

> Suicide is viewed by Muslims as taking away the gift of life given by God. The Qur'an says to trust God, have faith in the mercy of God, have patience, and not to destroy life. Suicide is viewed as an action resulting from psychological illness and severe life stresses. Although the act is not condoned, the person who dies by suicide is not condemned.[1]

> Taking your own life is viewed as a very serious violation of your responsibility to God and society if you are in your right mind, in part because it denies you the opportunity to repent. In Jewish law, there is no right to self-mutilation or suicide since you are only 'renting' your body from God. People who die by suicide cannot be buried inside a Jewish cemetery; spaces for them are reserved just outside the cemetery. … The Jewish law against suicide is only one narrow aspect of the far wider and more important idea that God loves humans without qualification and indeed created us uniquely in the Divine image. Jewish teachings never condone suicide, but Jews tend not to blame the person who dies by suicide.[2]

> Traditional Hindus believe in the immortality of the soul and in reincarnation. While death should not be feared, a human rebirth is rare and precious – and should not be ended prematurely. Because of 'karma,' a law of cause and effect, taking one's own life may lead to harmful consequences in the next incarnation(s).[3]

> Although Buddhism does not directly address suicide, it is based on non-violence – not killing or harming living things. Killing oneself is seen as a harmful action that will not end one's suffering but, rather,

---

[1] Action Alliance, 'Muslim', *Action Alliance*, https://theactionalliance.org/faith-hope-life/religion-specific-materials/muslim, accessed 08.04.2025.

[2] The National Action Alliance for Suicide Prevention, 'Suicide – The Jewish Perspective', *The Action Alliance*, https://theactionalliance.org/sites/default/files/2018_jewish_perspective_final.pdf, accessed 08.04.2025.

[3] The National Action Alliance for Suicide Prevention, 'Hinduism', *The Action Alliance*, https://theactionalliance.org/faith-hope-life/religion-specific-materials/hindu, accessed 08.04.2025.

lead to another form of suffering. Although Buddhists do not condone suicide, they do not condemn the person who dies by suicide. Rather, they focus on providing comfort to those bereaved.[4]

The story of suicide

We live our lives in stories – stories we make for ourselves, stories that we inherit from our culture or family, and stories we are sold by those seeking to influence us. When a person comes to a place in their heart and mind that leads them to contemplate taking their own life, it is often because they have been engulfed by a particular, sometimes sinister, invariably damaging and usually profoundly incorrect kind of story that leaves them feeling, 'I am worthless and life is hopeless.'

Sometimes a person is subject to a powerful, oppressive force over which they have no control, such as domestic, sexual or physical abuse, or bullying, prejudice or stigma, often rooted in attitudes to difference. Sometimes such pressure can be created or worsened by culture or faith traditions, for example in relation to sexuality or gender identity. Some people can feel trapped, with no way out, perhaps in debt, or in prison, or through the experience of homelessness. Some can be responding to a major life change, such as bereavement (including by suicide), redundancy, retirement, or the end of a relationship. Some can feel exhausted or desperate living with long-term pain or sickness. Some face mental health challenges, in some cases related to childbirth, or exacerbated by addiction or use of drugs. For some there is an overwhelming feeling of failure, isolation, inadequacy or worthlessness, exacerbated for many by social media. Others suffer the long-term after-effects of trauma, for example post-traumatic stress disorder after experiences of war or violence, which can surface many years after the events in question.

These are among a host of circumstances or conditions in which suicidal thoughts can arise. Many of them coalesce around a certain kind of story. One such story is that the world is simply atomic – the existence of life, beings, personalities and consciousness is accidental and not inevitable or purposeful, and that we are subject to the biochemical reactions generated by the food we eat, our naturally selected propensity to settle and procreate, and our external circumstances. It is

---

4 The National Action Alliance for Suicide Prevention, 'Buddhist', *The Action Alliance*, https://theactionalliance.org/faith-hope-life/religion-specific-materials/buddhist, accessed 08.04.2025.

not hard to feel lost, alone and meaningless in such a world. Another such story is that human existence is inherently competitive: we are essentially the same as we were before civilization became established – competing for resources, mates, opportunity, food, and all kinds of advantage. If then we see ourselves as a poor specimen, weak physically or struggling mentally, it's easy to inhabit a story in which we are useless or worse, where self-rejection and self-hatred can take over, and make us think we ought to jump off the back of the truck. A third such story is that there is purpose and meaning in existence, but that we've forfeited it by our failure, or been thwarted by another's hostility, or cannot in any way access it due to some less-defined inhibition. In such a story we can feel hopeless, abandoned and without any route back into the story, whether through our fault or another's, or due to bad luck or accident. The point is the main events in the story have happened, not to our advantage, and there's no prospect of changing them – and living with things as they are is beyond our capacity.

The Christian story offers a different account of all these things. It maintains there *is* a meaning and purpose – there always was and always will be. Things can indeed go badly, and people can experience hurt, failure, pain and abandonment. But God is with us, even and perhaps especially in those desolate times. Distress is not a sign that God has failed or that we have – that the world is against us or that there's no place for us in the story. In Christ, God experienced agonizing suffering but in that suffering we see God's resolve never to let us go, whatever befall. So hopelessness, helplessness and worthlessness are things most people experience some of the time and some people undergo most of the time. But the overall story is one of companionship, solidarity, hope and trust. We will finally, never be alone and we cannot, finally, ruin things beyond God's capacity to turn our failures into opportunities for deeper truth and more profound relationship.

The most profound words in the Bible are found in Song of Songs 8.6: 'Love is strong as death.' This is the question we find in the face of suicide: is love stronger than death? It certainly doesn't always feel like it. But Paul's words in Romans 8.38–39 provide the most stirring answer: 'I am convinced that neither death, nor life, nor angels, nor rulers, nor things present, nor things to come, nor powers, nor height, nor depth, nor anything else in all creation, will be able to separate us from the love of God in Christ Jesus our Lord.' In this chapter he speaks of 17 things that pose an almost insurmountable problem to being with God and sustaining faith in God; and the remarkable thing is that he'd experienced almost all of those things himself. He knew depression, despair, rejection, isolation, grief, doubt, pain. But in the end he trusted that love was stronger than death.

Christians die by suicide too. For all the same reasons as anyone else. And sometimes also because of the humiliation of realizing that being a Christian does not make them immune from all those things – particularly the shame of public exposure, should their life not have been all it may have seemed. But at the heart of the Christian story is the trust that God knows the secrets of all our hearts and isn't surprised by anything; nor does anything – anything whatsoever, including our own suicide – divert God from the commitment and desire to be in relationship with us forever.

Faith in the face of suicide

What are we to do when we feel despair and an urge to self-destruction? What are we to think and feel and do when facing the loss by suicide of someone we deeply loved?

God's purpose is to be with us, and for us to be with ourselves, one another and the wider creation now and forever. The most tangible way we can feel this is through our relationships with other people. Here are four such relationships.

The most fundamental is *being with*. In the book of Job, when terrible things befell him, Job's friends came to see him, and we're told, 'They sat with him on the ground for seven days and seven nights, and no one spoke a word to him, for they saw that his suffering was very great' (Job 2.13). The worst thing in the world is total isolation; and the best thing in the world is being with – genuine solidarity and companionship. You can get that from calling Samaritans – but in truth, someone you know well would very likely long to offer it to you.

There's a place for three other ways of relating. *Working with* usually takes time. It's where both parties have something important and complementary to bring to getting to a better place. One such relationship is with a counsellor, who through listening and support can enable you to find a new way of telling your story, a way that perhaps doesn't leave you feeling hopeless and worthless. Working with can also mean finding useful things to do with others, in which you can find pride and take pleasure from positively impacting others. *Working for* is also important. There can be medical and other professionals who through prescription of medicines or other changes or interventions can alter your state of mind in a way that can take away dark thoughts and overwhelming fears. *Being for* is more remote. It's probably for later – if you come out of this troubled time and are able to educate or advocate for a changed public awareness of these issues.

So much for one another. But being with God is also important. I think of prayer like this. Imagine an hourglass. In one half is what we might call essence: it lasts forever, it has no beginning or end, and in it all thoughts and actions are of limitless value in and of themselves – not for what result they may later produce, or estimation others might someday bestow on them. In the other half is existence: it lasts for a limited time, it is subject to flaw, fragility and failure, it is a realm where nothing is ever complete or perfect or fully understood or trusted. It is where we dwell. In between the two halves of the hourglass is an aperture. The name of that aperture is Jesus. Jesus is wholly of essence – forever – but becomes wholly also of existence – this world. Through him, existence perceives that essence is there, and what essence is like. Prayer is the name of the moment in our existence when we enter that aperture. We stand in our present existence – but in the light of eternal essence. We ask that existence to become more like essence (intercession). We lament that our own lives are far from that essence (confession). We marvel at essence (praise). And we express gratitude that there is existence at all, and for the moments in existence when we glimpse the wonder of essence (thanksgiving). As we do all these things we speak through Jesus – through the aperture to the essence. It is thus a conversation.

When we face utter despair, we can always pray in just this kind of way. Each of these four kinds of prayer can be transformative. Being with is the epicentre of prayer, because it's precisely the feeling of not being alone, not being abandoned, that addresses our biggest fear – isolation. But to pray seeking this condition of being with, and yet not to experience it, can leave one worse off than before – if it provides no sensation of being accompanied but, instead, failure or frustration. It's easy to say that the secret is not to go searching for God but gently to let the Holy Spirit come to you: while good advice, it's not straightforward or especially helpful counsel to follow should one be feeling desperate. Nonetheless, it's the goal of all prayer – to know that, as Jesus says, 'I am with you always, to the end of the age' (Matthew 28.20), and to feel that sense of presence and companionship. And it's the best thing in the world to feel that sense of solidarity and connectedness with another person – perhaps especially in the face of adversity, sadness or loss.

The prayer of working with breaks through isolation in a different way. It's about realizing there genuinely are some things one can do oneself – even though God must do what one can't. As the man at the foot of the Mount of Transfiguration put it, 'I believe; help my unbelief!' (Mark 9.24). It's about discovering, as Isaiah described, that an extra power can be accessed by those who let the Holy Spirit work through them: 'Those who wait for the Lord shall renew their strength, they shall mount up with wings like eagles, they shall run and not be weary, they shall walk and not faint' (Isaiah 40.31). It's about finding that what one could not do oneself, one has nonetheless found a way to do – as Paul puts it, '… though it was not I, but the grace of God that is with me' (1 Corinthians 15.10). Such partnership isn't always conscious. As the disciples on the way to Emmaus discovered, in their despair, the identity of their conversation partner wasn't immediately obvious: 'While they were talking and discussing, Jesus himself came near and went with them, but their eyes were kept from recognizing him' (Luke 24.15–16). The joy of partnership comes when we realize there are some things we can do, while accepting and celebrating that there are other things only God can do. When the disciples despair that there is nothing for 5,000 people to eat, it's they who find the meagre loaves and fishes, they who bring them to Jesus, they who distribute the remarkable result, and they who gather up twelve baskets of leftovers; but it's Jesus who actually does the miracle.

Working with has a second dimension beyond allowing God to work through and beside you. That is to find reward in partnering with another person or several other people. The point is not the goal but the satisfaction in addressing a project together. Facing adversity, overcoming obstacles, regrouping and re-envisioning, withstanding exhaustion, disagreeing over the best approach, forging trust and shared direction, achieving something together you couldn't have accomplished alone: these are profoundly restorative and renewing experiences that offer some of the best that life can provide. Sometimes, like the disciples reflecting on the Emmaus encounter, one can look back and say, 'Were not our hearts burning within us?' (Luke 24.32) – because the partnership was so intense that one lost oneself in it. Such a moment of losing oneself can be profoundly inspiring and therapeutic. But it is still not always enough.

Working for is a more familiar kind of prayer and encounter. This is where some external party fixes the problem, or seeks to. It's how we most often think of prayer – asking or pleading with God to do something to make a bad situation better. When people say they've lost their faith, it's commonly because they have besought God to heal a person, yet that person has not been healed – and so they say, 'What's the use?' While in grief we search for explanations and are inclined to lay blame, but such a vision is an impoverished notion of God and of prayer. Prayer is not placing ourselves at the centre of the story and demanding God fix our problem like a servant leaping into action at our behest. It is becoming aware of the mystery of grace by which we come to exist and realizing how precious is life, our world, our relationships, ourselves and the body, mind and spirit we've been given, and discovering something of the source and purpose of all these things.

Nonetheless, there are three dimensions of working for that can be helpful. In looking to God to alleviate our cause of distress, we are opening our lives to change, and ceasing to regard our situation as utterly hopeless and pointless. In seeking help from another party, especially a doctor or other medical professional, we are likewise moving from supposing our situation is uniquely and unchangeably insoluble to a position where we accept our predicament is subject to change and improvement. And perhaps, most transformatively, if we accept that God or someone else can 'work for' us by addressing our problems, we may realize that we too can do something similar for others. It can be in such moments of discovery – often simple things that cost us little or nothing, but make a tremendous difference to others – that we can begin to find the purpose and value that had deserted us. To find one's identity in making a difference in others' lives isn't a whole ethic – but it's indescribably better than feeling we are worthless, life is pointless, the future is hopeless, and we'd better not be here.

One form this activity can take is to seek to advocate for and inform the public about others who find themselves in such a crisis. Being for is a way to describe activities that raise awareness about suicide or seek to make early interventions among people who might be the last to let on that anything was amiss. Being for doesn't itself involve relationship with a person in the midst of despair – but it can nonetheless be a constructive way of channelling regret, sadness, bitterness and grief that enhances the lives of those who face painful feelings and thoughts. It can be a fine way to turn the experience of having come close to ending one's life into assisting others in similar situations – or their relatives and friends. And being for is the essence of praying for others: bringing before God the names and experiences of those who are in trouble, and reflecting before God on others who may be keeping their struggles a secret.

These words about prayer, and about how prayer and action coalesce, are not intended to suggest that prayer is the answer to any and all experiences of contemplating suicide. They are simply a way to frame how we may configure suicide, whether as one who is considering taking our own life, one supporting a person in such a situation, or a person trying to find a way through in the aftermath of losing a loved one. Suicide confronts us with issues of eternity and powerlessness: and this is precisely the territory that prayer occupies.

10

Ideas for Preparing Your Own 'Time Together' Service

ANN FELOY

Getting the balance right: Everyone is welcome

My hope is that this chapter provides you and your team with sufficient information to run your own 'Time Together' service at your cathedral, church, place of worship or other public venue.

The event marks its tenth anniversary in 2025. It would be wonderful for 'Time Together' services to spread their wings and take place at the same time in other parts of Britain, and perhaps around the world; although in some cases it may not be possible or desirable to hold the event close to Suicide Prevention Day, and there may be other significant occasions to mark. I hope that even more people affected by suicide will gather together to experience fellowship, compassion and understanding. The service is designed to welcome everyone of all backgrounds, no matter what their religion, or if they are of no professed faith. Everyone is invited who is looking for comfort and healing.

In this chapter there is an example of a 'Time Together' programme and also suggestions for music, poems and readings you might like to include. The aim is to have a balance of beautiful music – either sung or instrumental – as well as spoken word in the form of prose, poetry or readings. One well-known hymn is also included in the service at St Martin's. No prayers, such as the Lord's Prayer, are said, however, as the event is non-religious and non-denominational. If you are holding this service at a place of worship, no matter what denomination, you may like to consider including some prayers or more music or songs of a spiritual nature.

The programme is merely a guide. It is up to you and your team to decide how closely you wish to follow the St Martin's format. However, we hope you will find the three-part structure helpful, in order to create a sensitive, supportive and safe event. We have found that members of the congregation feel a sense of security from the familiar, contained format of the service in which speakers share their very personal and moving stories.

When is the service held and how long does it last?

The 'Time Together' service takes place at 2pm on the Saturday nearest World Suicide Prevention Day, 10 September. The service lasts one hour and is followed by refreshments for those who want to stay on afterwards. This allows for those who have gathered to meet others with similar experiences of loss or struggles with mental health.

What is the structure of the service?

The words and music accompany a shared journey in three parts, which are represented by the symbolic gesture of either a rock, candle or rose being placed on a small table in front of the lectern before the speaker gives their testimony.

I. Lost. Laying a rock.

The music, testimony and readings in this first section are represented by the first speaker placing a rock, representing the hardest path of all to tread at the moment of despair or heartbreak.

II. In the Valley. Lighting a candle.

The music, testimony and readings in the second section are represented by lighting a candle, which symbolizes a dark and deep-sided valley with a glimmer of a light up ahead to guide us through the pain.

III. Found. Placing a rose.

The music, testimonies and readings in this third and final section are represented by a rose, reflecting the nurturing and perhaps even blooming of acceptance, healing and hope.

IDEAS FOR PREPARING YOUR OWN 'TIME TOGETHER' SERVICE

What happens before the service?

People are welcomed by ushers and handed a programme as they arrive. Members of the congregation start to take their seats up to an hour before the service begins so that they can sit quietly and gather their thoughts. During this time, they are invited to place a small stone and/or a rose on the altar and/or light a votive candle to resonate with their feelings of upset or grief. Taking part in this gesture allows all those present to play their part in the service and connect with the three themes. The visual effect of the roses and candles is powerful, and remains in the memory long after the day.

Who speaks during the service?

The vicar and organizer give a welcome and an address at the start of the service, which together last ten minutes. In the case of St Martin's, this is given by Revd Dr Sam Wells and Ann Feloy, founder and CEO of the charity Olly's Future. During the service, four speakers read their written testimonies, which last no more than five minutes each. Sometimes other speakers read out a poem or a piece of prose to reflect the different themes of the service.

In total the spoken word takes up around 30 minutes, which is the same amount of time as the musical performances.

How do you choose the speakers to give a testimony?

At every service, we hear from four speakers who have either lost loved ones to suicide or else have attempted to take their own life. It may be that you already know some people who you feel would have the strength and courage to speak about their experiences. Other people may be able to suggest people they have previously heard speak.

In order to give equal weight to each person's story, speakers are asked to read out a five-minute testimony. While some speakers may feel they want to find the words on the day, this is not encouraged as it can be extremely emotional for the person giving their testimony. Having their words written in front of them can give them confidence and reassure the organizers that the service will maintain the right sensitive-but-not-immersed emotional balance.

The organizer should ideally meet the person giving a testimony, or at least speak to them on the phone or have an online meeting to get an idea of what they will be speaking about. It will then become clear where the testimony sits best in the order of the service in relation to the three themes.

Ask those giving a testimony to send you their piece of writing in advance for you to create the running order of the programme. It is important that speakers arrive at least 15 minutes before the service begins so that you can meet them and settle any nerves. They should be seated together at the front of the church so that it is easy for them to come to the lectern to speak. Ensure microphones are on and any recording equipment is working.

Who performs the music at the service?

This is entirely up to you and your team. At St Martin's, Director of Music Andrew Earis puts together an exquisite repertoire sung by St Martin's Voices. You may have an ensemble that can perform throughout the service or you may choose to invite singers to perform who are not attached to the place of worship or venue. The repertoire at St Martin's is predominantly English classical but you may wish to bring a different feel to your 'Time Together' service.

Are there any safeguarding issues to consider?

We always have at least three people on hand who can speak to anyone who feels upset and needs to leave during the service. At the beginning, the organizer should point out that there are trained counsellors at the back of the congregation who can offer emotional support to anyone who needs to talk or needs to take a breath.

Is it OK to take photographs and film the service?

It is essential that those people attending feel that they are in a safe environment. Often people will cry or be upset. The last thing they want is to be filmed. For these reasons it is important that no photography or filming takes place. It is worth the organizer setting this out in their welcome.

IDEAS FOR PREPARING YOUR OWN 'TIME TOGETHER' SERVICE

It may be that the venue where you hold the 'Time Together' service can make a professional audio or video recording, if this is agreeable to those reading testimonies and performing the music.

What artwork is there if we choose to run a 'Time Together' Service?

We have used three logos: the 'Time Together' logo of a multi-coloured tulip, designed by Oli Mosse; the St Martin-in-the-Fields logo; and the Olly's Future logo. This artwork is available from Olly's Future for use in social media and promotional material if helpful.

Should we charge an entrance fee?

This is entirely up to you and depends on the costs that you need to meet. You may be able to run the event without charging admission if your costs are low. In the case of the London event, we offer free tickets via Eventbrite, but also invite people to make a donation in advance when they book their place via the ticketing platform. On the day we also ask people to help us cover the costs of the hire of the venue and the musicians, as well as the cost of the reception area and the refreshments. We have baskets for cash, card readers and envelopes in pews. A QR code to make a payment is included in the programme.

Another way that Olly's Future is able to raise some money towards the costs of the event is by asking well-known and well-loved charities in the bereavement sector to support the event with a stand. We charge according to the size of the organization. It is so important to feel you are connecting with other charities doing wonderful work in the field of suicide bereavement.

How long does it take to plan the event?

It is surprising how long it takes to plan the service. There is a lot of work to do. You will need a small close-knit team to make the service beautiful on the day. It is one of our flagship events of the year at Olly's Future and takes a minimum of six months to arrange, even though the event has been established at St Martin's for a decade.

Ideally you should allow a year to start planning the event from scratch. Hopefully some of the hard work of thinking about when to hold the event, the structure and the artwork, as well as suggestions for music and poems, has been done for you in this guide.

What happens after the service?

Immediately following the service we invite everyone to join us for refreshments in another area where there is space to mingle. This offers people the chance to talk to others about their experiences, to share their stories of loss and to feel a powerful connection with others who have suffered equally. It is a very positive atmosphere, full of compassion and often laughter.

Suicide bereavement charities supporting the event have stands offering advice, literature and resources to those at the reception. It is a wonderful testament to those working in this field that they come together to support this event.

Not everyone stays on after the service. Perhaps half the ground-floor capacity 550 congregation at St Martin's leave straightaway, preferring not to stay for refreshments. Often, in the wake of a tragic loss, it is extremely hard to summon the energy to talk to others, especially strangers. It is enough just to be part of a service of mutual understanding, to listen and reflect.

Sample outline

Choral 'Lean on Me', Bill Withers
'You Are The Reason', Calum Scott

Instrumental 'Farewell to Stromness', Peter Maxwell Davies

Welcome Remarks

Address

Anthem *'Ubi caritas'*, Ola Gjeilo

IDEAS FOR PREPARING YOUR OWN 'TIME TOGETHER' SERVICE

I. Lost
Laying a rock

Testimony

Song 'Alternate Reality – Darragh's Song', Josh Smith

Poem 'Adrift', Mark Nepo

Silent Reflection

Anthem *Agnus Dei II* from *Missa Brevis*, Palestrina, arr. Becky McGlade

II. The Valley
Lighting a candle

Choral 'We shall walk through the valley in peace', spiritual arr. Undine Smith Moore

Testimony

Piano solo Menuet from *Le Tombeau de Couperin*, Maurice Ravel

Testimony

III. Found
Placing a rose

Solo 'Gabriel's Oboe', Ennio Morricone

Testimony

Choral 'O love', Elaine Hagenberg

Poem 'Sing Their Name', Catherine McCusker

Choral 'Rise Up', Andra Day

Hymn 'Lord of all hopefulness, Lord of all joy', Jan Struther

Closing remarks
The programme includes a thank you to all those suicide bereavement charities who support the event. We list their contact details and helplines.

Welcome

Here are some ideas on how you can give a welcome address to those attending.

Welcome to this very unique gathering. It is our 'time together', as the name suggests, to connect with those whose lives have been affected by suicide. This is a non-denominational and non-religious service, for people of different faiths or none. Everyone is welcome.

I hope this service provides a gentle and compassionate place, where you feel you are among others with a shared understanding of how hard life can be, but also how important it is to cherish all you have.

Since 2015 there has been an annual service hosted by Revd Dr Sam Wells at St Martin-in-the-Fields on Trafalgar Square, London for those affected by suicide. While we gather here, hundreds of people are gathering at St Martin's, and our service follows the same format.

There are three parts to this service. They are symbolized by the stone, representing the hardest path of all to tread and the dark night of the soul; the candle, representing a light at the end of the deepest of valleys to guide you through; and finally a rose – the nurturing and perhaps even blooming of acceptance, healing and hope.

Alternative version

Thank you for sharing your time with us here today by coming to this service for those affected by suicide, whether having lost someone in the most tragic of ways or having struggled with thoughts of suicide yourself. You are with others who understand your pain and sadness, even though they may be complete strangers. I hope those who placed a stone or a rose on the altar, and/or lit a votive candle before the service, found this comforting.

The service falls as close to World Suicide Prevention Day on 10 September as possible. The name 'Time Together' recognizes the shared connection in simply being together and being part of a group that understands the greatest depths of suffering to humankind – deeper than words. Sometimes just gathering together is enough. Finding the energy to mingle and talk can be too hard.

My hope is that this service gives you a moment to pause and look into your heart and reflect on your experience. We will hear the testi-

IDEAS FOR PREPARING YOUR OWN 'TIME TOGETHER' SERVICE

monies of people who have either been bereaved by suicide or else had thoughts of ending their own life but have found the strength and courage to share their stories. We'll also listen to music by …

I hope it also gives you a chance to contemplate the enormity of all that you have faced, the insights that you have gained and perhaps, somewhere in among that, the blessings that you have been granted.

Finally, a gentle reminder not to take photographs or video but rather to immerse yourself in the words and music.

Thank you for sharing this time with us in love and fellowship.

Musical suggestions

O Paalanhaare, Javed Akhtar
'Crossing the Bar', Rani Arbo
Geistliches Lied, Op. 30, Johannes Brahms
'Sea of Solitude' (*Seafaring Folk*: Movement V), Jonathan Brigg
Agnus Dei, William Byrd
'The Lord's my shepherd', Bob Chilcott
'Upon your heart', Eleanor Daley
'Farewell to Stromness', Peter Maxwell Davies
'Rise Up', Andra Day
Cantique de Jean Racine, Gabriel Fauré
Pavane, Gabriel Fauré
Ubi caritas, Ola Gjeilo
'In Peace Eternal', Sharon Grenham-Thompson, Alison Willis
'My Companion', Elaine Hagenburg
'O love', Elaine Hagenberg
'You do not walk alone', Elaine Hagenberg
'O Thou that art the light', Gabriel Jackson
Kyrie from *Missa Brevis*, Zoltán Kodály
'Gabriel's Oboe', Ennio Morricone
Agnus Dei II from *Missa Brevis*, Palestrina, arr. Becky McGlade
Da Pacem Domine, Arvo Part
Dido's Lament from *Dido and Aeneas*, Henry Purcell
Chaconne in G Minor, Henry Purcell
Menuet from *Le Tombeau de Couperin* (piano solo), Maurice Ravel
'A Prayer of St Patrick', John Rutter
'The Lord Bless You and Keep You', John Rutter
'The Lord is My Shepherd', John Rutter

'You Are The Reason', Calum Scott
'We shall walk through the valley in peace', Undine Smith Moore (arr.)
'The Beatitudes', Philip Stopford
'The Lamb', John Tavener
'Lean on Me', Bill Withers
'There is a Balm in Gilead', traditional spiritual

Suggested poems and readings

'After Great Pain, a Formal Feeling Comes', Emily Dickinson
'Snowdrops' from *The Wild Iris*, Louise Gluck
'I have desired to go', Gerard Manley Hopkins
'Carry a Whisper', Jola Malin
'Adrift', Mark Nepo
'Yes, We Can Talk', Mark Nepo
'On the Death of the Beloved', John O'Donohue
'Time to be Slow', John O'Donohue
'Blessed are you who bear the light', Jan Richardson
'The Echo of Silence', Rumi
'Blessing for One Who Has Taken Their Own Life', David Whyte
'The Sacrament of Waiting', Macrina Wiederkehr

Hymn suggestions

'Abide with Me', Henry Francis Lyte
'Lord of All Hopefulness', Jan Struther
'Be Still My Soul', Catharina von Schlegel, trans. Jane Borthwick

11

Personal and Public Prayers

SAMUEL WELLS

This chapter offers prayers for different contexts relating to the possibility, prospect or aftermath of a person – known and loved, or oneself – taking their own life. The prayers are set out in the form of a collect and thus have five sections: an address to God, a context in which the petition seems justified, the change sought, the anticipated result of the change, and the means used. They're set in the context of Christian conviction, but can be adapted for other purposes. Some are for personal use; others for a service such as the annual service that inspired this book, or perhaps a funeral or memorial service.

Personal prayers

Pain

God of compassion, in Christ you wept with the daughters of Jerusalem. Be with me as I face pain too hard for me to endure. By your Holy Spirit, create in me strength, patience and endurance, that I may find a way to go on, and be some kind of blessing to others. In Christ who knew agony but in whom others find hope. Amen.

Hurt

Tender God, your Son endured his friends' flight, denial and betrayal. Comfort me as I struggle with what others have done to me and the state I find myself in. Assuage my agony, lift me up through my desolation, and heal my wounds, that in this time of hurt and injury I may come to know myself more fully and yourself more truly. In Christ your wounded healer. Amen.

Meaninglessness

Truthful God, your Son's followers turned away from him when they didn't know who to trust. Hold my hand when I can't see the point of life, existence, or going on. Visit me by your Holy Spirit in my places of despair, depression and desolation. When I walk through the valley of the shadow of death, let me find your Son walking beside me. And give me compassion for others who feel as bleak as I do. In Christ who dwelt in the wilderness and was so alone. Amen.

Hopelessness

Sustaining God, your Son's friends Nicodemus and Joseph of Arimathea carried his body to the tomb on the day of his death. Send a pillar of cloud to guide me by day and a pillar of fire to guide me by night. When the way ahead seems hopeless and impossible, send your Holy Spirit to enable me to put one foot in front of the other. Make me see the beauty in the miniature and the dignity in the simple, that each day turns from one of despair to one of possibility. In Christ you make all things new: transform me from the shadows into the dawn. Through Christ our risen Lord. Amen.

Shame

Embracing God, your Son said to the woman about to be stoned, 'I do not condemn you.' Meet me in my place of fear – of exposure, of ridicule, of having no leg to stand on. By your Holy Spirit, relocate my identity from my own accomplishments to my belonging in you. Protect me from the hurtfulness of things people say and the pain of rejection by those who once respected me. And make this the beginning of something truer and more faithful. In Christ who sees me for what I am and still loves me. Amen.

Guilt

God in whom the future is always bigger than the past, you see who we are and you love what you have made. Send your Holy Spirit to sift through our sorrow and guilt about the past. Turn those things we deeply regret into sources of wisdom and understanding that may benefit ourselves and others. Transform those things that shroud and burden us into reasons for compassion and grace. As you brought resurrection out of death, make something beautiful out of so many sad things today. In Christ who turned Peter from denier to rock of your people. Amen.

Wretchedness

God of forever, your servant Job wished he had never been born. Be close to me in my utter despair. Let me feel your understanding, your compassion and your solidarity when I feel I have nowhere to turn and I can't bear to face each new day. As your people built a new city and temple out of the ruins of Jerusalem, send your Holy Spirit to turn the valley of my dry bones into the beginning of your new hope. In Christ our resurrected Lord. Amen.

Confusion

God of love, your Son Jesus came to his disciples across the stormy waters. When my mind is scrambled, when I forget who I am and where I belong, take my hand, precious Lord, and lead me on. When I face storms without and chaos within, show me a way ahead. And send me companions when I am utterly lost, that I may find my way home. In Christ who calmed the storm. Amen.

Recklessness

Unwavering God, your Son Jesus stayed true to his purpose despite fear and agony. I am frightened of what I might do to myself when I think it would be easier for everyone if I were gone. When I tread the verge of Jordan, bid my anxious fears subside. When I lose control of my heart and mind, support me by your Spirit and send me companions to watch out for me. Lift my spirits through the beauty, the wonder and the glory of your created world. And give me strength for another day. In Christ who at his moment of weakness found Simon of Cyrene able to share his burden. Amen.

Horror

God of enduring love, in Jesus you dared to look into the tomb even though Lazarus had been dead four days. Be with me when I face truths and hurts and horrors greater than I think I can bear. Walk with me when I stumble, stay with me when I can't keep still, and wait with me when I want to run away, that I may find in you a reason for living and strength to keep going. Make me a person of courage and endurance, that I may never give up; and make of me a person with whom others know they never walk alone. In Christ whom Stephen beheld even as he faced his own death. Amen.

Public prayers

Sadness

Mysterious God, you have taken away from us one we didn't ever want to be without, one whose absence makes our lives feel empty, and yet one whose life has invigorated and inspired a thousand lives. Take today our sadness, grief and desolation and make of them something of hope and beauty and consolation, that even as we mourn the loss of this our loved one, we cherish all the more the wonders that you brought into the world through them. In the one who leads us through death to everlasting life.

Despair

God of meaning and purpose, without our lost loved one we wonder what the point is of all things, where to find hope, how to carry on. Show us your grace in the tender beauties and intricate wonders of existence; lift our hearts by the kindness of strangers and the goodness of friends; and renew us by the abiding gift of what this person gave us in spirit and in truth.

Loss

God of life, we stand before you in dismay at the loss of one who brought so much life. Turn our grief to truer living, our sadness to firmer hope, and our sorrow to deeper joy. Walk with those closest to this person that they may find strength and consolation and companions to face each new day without them. In your Holy Spirit, never let us go.

Dismay

God of love, in you love is stronger than death. Heal our pain of loss; lift our burden of desolation; be close to us in the valley of the shadow of fear and despair. Remake our loved one out of all the love they embodied among us; and keep them in your heart forever.

Bewilderment

God of wonder, your people spent 40 years in the wilderness. When we can't be happy, you make our lives beautiful. Turn our perception of scarcity into discovery of your abundance. When we don't know what to trust, and feel our whole world has been upended, give us tasks to do, people to be close to, and new skills to learn, that even if our hearts are heavy, you may fill our days with purpose and hope.

Rage

Faithful God, your Son upturned tables and gave vent to your rage. When our hearts are engulfed by fury, show us where to direct our anger and powerlessness. Where people have failed us and let us down, teach us how to hold them accountable in ways that are just and dignified. Where those who have hurt us are no longer alive, give us channels for our energy and passion. Turn our helplessness into your way of transforming the world, that even as we feel useless and timid, you may work through us to bring liberation and belonging.

Gratitude

Wondrous God, your Son showed us how you decorate even the lilies of the field. Lift our hearts and minds so that we see beauty where we might miss it; raise our spirits that we find appreciation where we might harbour only resentment; and open our eyes to see the glory of your created existence: that through your Holy Spirit our despair may turn to enthralment and our disillusion become enchantment.

Truth

Merciful God, your Son promised the truth would set us free. Surround us with the everlasting arms of your Spirit's love and care, that as we face things we'd rather not know and discover things that change what we thought we could trust, you lead us to a peace that passes all understanding. Give us compassionate hearts and farsighted understanding, that even as we only partly know, we may trust that in you we are fully known.

Fear

God of grace, in Christ you promise never to leave us or abandon us. Walk with us when we are terrified. Give us strength to face the prospect of death, the fear of the unknown, the possibility of pain and the terror of isolation. Write on our hearts your words of faithfulness and hope, that we may walk towards our greatest fears, and discover with wonder that we are truly walking towards you.

Blessing

God bless you; when your heart is broken, may God the Father's heart be open to you; when your hands are in pain, may God the Son's scars appear to you; when you walk through the valley of the shadow of death, may God the Holy Spirit walk beside you, that you may always know that with God, you need never be alone.

Appendix: Reflective Practices

There follow practices and reflections for different contexts relating to the possibility, prospect, or aftermath of a person – known and loved, or oneself – taking their own life. The practices may seem glib to some, helpful to others: they are not a panacea or a cure, but designed to be positive ways to find a path out of despair.

1. Finding meaning amid emptiness

Try to focus on one thing – maybe your finger, maybe a pen or an item of food or clothing. Then do two things. (1) First expand from it – imagine yourself zooming out from it, from this table on which it rests, this kitchen in which the table sits, this house in which the kitchen is found, this street, this neighbourhood, this town, this region, this country, this continent, this planet ... and keep zooming out through solar system and galaxy and universe, as slowly as you can while keeping your concentration. Then, when you've zoomed out as far as your imagination can take you, reverse the process and zoom in as slowly as you're able, until you reach the original frame and size. (2) Then keep going, into the item itself, going down through particles, molecules, elements, nuclei, electrons and so on, as far as your remembered biology or imagined speculation can take you. Then linger as previously, before zooming back, stage by stage, to the original frame and size. This is an exercise to find meaning in detail, texture, extent, and thereby find perspective and ultimately wonder. It's an attempt to overcome the glazed stupor of the one for whom all things have become the same and without significance or purpose, and to replace that dullness with an intricate engagement with mysterious interconnection.

2. Finding hope amid despair

Try to recall – by writing down if helpful, on paper or screen – some of the worst experiences of your life, as simply and unsentimentally as possible. Then, against each one, record what happened next – how you found a way to go on, how you found strength and purpose and companionship and didn't let the adverse circumstance have the last word. Then try to do the same exercise for the worst things that have happened in the world – the Holocaust, the tsunamis, the genocides, wars, earthquakes and horrors that have scarred civilization – and again identify how people found a way to go on. This is an exercise in rediscovering the resilience of the human spirit and resources in oneself one didn't know (or had forgotten) one had. The point is not to deny how terrible you currently feel, but to remember that things can change, have changed, and will change, sometimes by your own efforts, other times by the efforts of others or through luck, surprise or accident.

3. Finding relationship amid isolation

Draw a family tree pointing out how you connect with everyone else in your wider family. Then draw a more complex tree of the people you know, whether you respect and trust them or not, and how they know each other or how they relate to one another. Imagine them all coming together at your funeral and both the known and surprising connections they might make with one another should they get talking – both their connection with you and some independent links they might have. This is an exercise in realizing how textured and supple are the web of relationships around each one of us, and how immense is the sum total of all those connections and bonds. While some of those relationships might be soured or severed, it may be that some are simply dormant – and some of those people would be delighted to reconnect, if not for your sake then maybe for theirs.

4. Finding identity amid powerlessness

Again, there are two dimensions to this exercise. (1) Who you are. Make a list of all your identities – offspring, parent, sibling, cousin, neighbour, plus profession, sports team supporter, gender/sexuality, convictions (whether political or social or religious), nationality, race or ethnicity, and so on. (2) What you do. Make a list of both everyday and less conventional actions you perform, from brushing your teeth to posting on social media – and against each action try to assess the number of people it might affect. For example, brushing your teeth might affect those who made, transported, advertised and sold your toothbrush and toothpaste, those who brought water to your bathroom and constructed and installed the basin, floor, walls and ceiling, your dentist, hygienist and so many more people. Your tiniest action can affect an enormous web of people. Your more significant actions at work or online can affect an enormous number more. Your identity is made up of who you are and the significance of what you do – and it is immensely detailed and textured. This is about appreciating and discovering an identity not limited to the labels others put on you or you bestow on yourself.

5. Finding trust after betrayal

If you find that a person you love and rely on is not the person you thought them to be, you may fear that trust can never be restored or even found elsewhere: whether it was a betrayal; whether they have done or are doing something you find intolerable; or in fact are something you never realized and cannot exist alongside; or if you have to face the fact that you have done something, or become someone, that has undermined or wrecked an interconnected web of precious and vulnerable ties. This requires a whole series of actions, some to address the damage done in the past, some to face up to the hurt existing in the present, and others to work on better patterns of relating and acting so as to ensure a different kind of future. These will benefit from talking through with another person and disentangling the emotions and conflicting impulses involved. But they will also need a calm, unsentimental inventory of what you have learned about yourself, what you need to cope and survive, and what new commitments to yourself and others you will need to put in place to avoid simply falling into the same situation again. Central among all these processes and resolutions is the determination not to see this thing that's happened to you, or that you've done, as the defining feature of your life and the location of your core identity; but to begin to see it as an important but not fundamental part of who you are.

6. Finding a way to go on after loss

When you have lost something integral to your sense of self, identity, well-being and existence – a person you loved, a relationship, a form of life or work, a home, an attachment or habit – it may well seem overwhelming; like something that touches everything else. The phrase 'This too is true' may seem idle or irrelevant: but it may become a lifesaver. Grief is about, on the one hand, allowing yourself to be sad – remembering good things, recognizing how much of your life was tied up in what's gone, struggling to get out from under the weight of confusion, sorrow and bewilderment; but also, on the other hand, about finding good and true things that have a validity independent of the loved one – a person they didn't know who is kind, interesting and faithful, a place they'd never been that is rewarding and fascinating, an event they never knew about that requires from you a response of resilience or resourcefulness. It's not a zero-sum game – both columns can be full at the same time – but the vital thing to recall is that you're not honouring the person you've lost by laying before their altar the sacrifice of your own misery. Their blessing to you is to enable you to live without them.

7. Finding forgiveness amid regret

It's completely natural and understandable to blame yourself and to speculate in detail over things you could have done differently that might have led to different outcomes for other people – especially if one of those other people has taken their own life. This is a common aspect of grief and not something to be suppressed or denied. It's not always completely untrue, either. Some regrets are real, genuine and lasting. The key is to find a way to live with regrets when the person from whom you're seeking forgiveness is no longer around to offer it. Besides trying to make penance by doing a beautiful thing in the person's honour, two other practices may be helpful. One is to try to make an exhaustive list of what you feel you have done wrong – as detailed and extensive as you feel able to, since this is meant to be a cathartic practice – and then to make a fire and burn it to cinders. (If it's your tradition, you may wish first to find a priest and read the list out to them and ask for forgiveness from God.) Another way is to find a trusted companion (or priest) and go through an imaginative exercise in your mind by which you load

APPENDIX: REFLECTIVE PRACTICES

up a boat with all the things you regret and when you're done, let that boat sail down a tributary into a river and watch it sail into the current and out into the sea until it's far away – and thus let those things you profoundly regret become part of all the wrongs done in the world and indistinguishable from them all; and thus no longer yours.

8. Finding peace amid anger

Anger is closely linked to powerlessness. It can be directed at another person, at oneself, or with less focus but just as much intensity at something beyond – God, life, the system. Anger can be a gift if it motivates and empowers you to do something constructive that overcomes your powerlessness and mitigates injustice or assists victims. But it can become sulphurous if it's allowed to spill into rage or fury, in which the intoxication of the feeling becomes like a self-justifying drug and self-fulfilling indulgence. There can be distinct and effective steps to move through anger to peace – usually involving the passage of time, the adoption of specific constructive actions, and the finding of solidarity with others afflicted. But again, it's usually counterproductive to try to suppress or ignore anger because it will invariably be stored up for later or emerge in other ways, including depression.

9. Finding a story amid devastation

'A story' might seem a little placid or lame compared to the searing intensity of emotions surrounding suicide; but sometimes suicide is closely connected either to the sense of pointlessness, meaninglessness and hopelessness, which could all be described as finding oneself without a story, or to some kind of false story that one doesn't matter, isn't loved, is a complete failure or can never be forgiven, any or all of which could be retold if only the person were able to open themselves out to be listened to by others and to realize for themselves how untrue such stories are. The experience of counselling or therapy is essentially about finding a way to assemble the dispersed and disparate elements of a shattered life or destroyed confidence into a story to live by, one that makes good-enough and empowering sense of words, experiences and events that had seemed overwhelming, incoherent or threatening. The challenge is to find the courage to put into words things that can seem horrifying, humiliating, terrifying or agonizing. Such things can't be rushed, but are the path towards life.

10. Allowing oneself to be found

The mistake in reviewing practices such as these is to regard them as forms of self-help. There's a place for self-help in restoring dignity and confidence and appropriate independence to go on. But the problem with self-help is that it can encourage a mindset that thinks we're fundamentally isolated individuals and we should try not to be a burden to anyone or risk rejection by sharing the truth about our lives with anyone. Sometimes finding belonging, trust and hope is about stopping running away – no longer deftly changing the subject when it becomes personal or tender, no longer withdrawing from relationships when they become real and intimate, no longer turning aside from another person's truth lest it make one face one's own. The heart of the despair that often leads to suicide is isolation – and the recipe for overcoming isolation is receiving the gift of one another. People need people: it's not a sign of weakness – it's the way things are supposed to be. No one is an island – everyone is a part of the mainland. Sometimes the beginning of health and healing is as simple as staying still and not turning or rushing away when someone begins truly to see you and what you're going through.

www.ingramcontent.com/pod-product-compliance
Lightning Source LLC
Chambersburg PA
CBHW060610080526
44585CB00013B/759